## Teacher's Edition

Bob Jones University Press, Greenville, South Carolina 29614

## Introduction

The Bob Jones University Press Bible Modular Series provides great flexibility for the Christian educator. At the beginning of the year, the teacher chooses the particular modular titles suited to the needs of the students. Each book contains readings, assignments, exercises, and tests for about one quarter of the academic year. The teacher then selects the materials within the book that will have the greatest impact on the students. See the BJUP catalog or www.bjup.com for titles currently available.

## Philosophy

*That I May Know Him* is not a commentary but rather a tool to teach students about Jesus Christ by using the Gospel of Mark. Teaching Bible is similar to other educational fields in that students progress through a series of learning stages. Each stage should have age-appropriate goals, objectives, and learning activities. Most elementary-age children trust their teachers and can readily learn the facts and simple applications of Scripture. On the other hand, most high school students pass through periods of doubt, questioning almost everything.

*That I May Know Him* is designed to encourage teens to think about and to internalize the words and work of Christ. For that reason, the book is not organized chronologically. Christ's message to a different group of people is presented in each chapter. The students

NOTE:

The fact that materials produced by other publishers may be referred to in this volume does not constitute an endorsement of the content or theological position of materials produced by such publishers. Any references and ancillary materials are listed as an aid to the student or the teacher and in an attempt to maintain the accepted academic standards of the publishing industry.

**That I May Know Him Teacher's Edition**

H. Douglas Garland, M.A.

**Editor:** Catherine Anderson
**Designer:** John Bjerk
**Composition:** Jennifer Hearing and Rebecca G. Zollinger

Photograph credits appear on page 132.

© 2002 Bob Jones University Press
Greenville, South Carolina 29614

Printed in the United States of America
All rights reserved

ISBN 1-57924-691-5

15 14 13 12 11 10 9 8 7 6 5 4 3

learn the facts by reading the text of Mark and through in-class exercises. The textbook then deals with the interpretation and the application of Mark to modern teens. The Teacher's Edition contains several suggestions to help the students understand Christ's claims on their lives.

## Practice

*That I May Know Him* is designed to help the instructor guide the students to a living relationship with Jesus Christ. Each chapter contains clearly stated goals and objectives, which should be reviewed prior to teaching the material. The reading of Mark is encouraged as a homework assignment and as an in-class exercise. The Appendix contains many suggestions to make the reading interesting. Optional memory verses are also provided. The students should be required to memorize some of the verses. Lesson plans based on a five-day cycle per chapter are included and may be modified as needed.

## Activities

Both the student and teacher editions contain numerous exercises and classroom activities. The teacher should choose the assignments best suited to the class's time and needs. It is best for the teacher to prepare well in advance of class time. Some activities require the students to read or to research a topic outside of class. A reasonable amount of homework will prepare students for outside work in college. Some schools require a project or

# CONTENTS

paper for Bible classes. Many of the assignments in *That I May Know Him* can be expanded into projects.

The purpose of the course is to challenge students with the message of Jesus Christ. Classroom procedures and practices should reflect the purpose. Include a variety of lecture, discussion, personal testimony, group projects, individual projects, and special speakers. The group projects in particular encourage creative thinking and student interaction. Set conduct standards for the group work. Control the class by giving clear instructions and by checking on the progress of each team. Choose and modify the activities as appropriate for the class.

Several exercises encourage use of the Internet. The class can be a vehicle to teach the students how to use the Internet properly and how to avoid offensive materials. Always follow church and school policies.

**Tests**

The Teacher's Edition contains two complete tests that may be modified as desired. The tests cover only information in the Student Text. Give points for class participation. Consider grading at least some of the exercises. The chapter review questions may be used for quizzes. Prepare the students for the future by including both objective and essay questions. The ability to formulate a well-reasoned response is an important leadership skill. Setting a

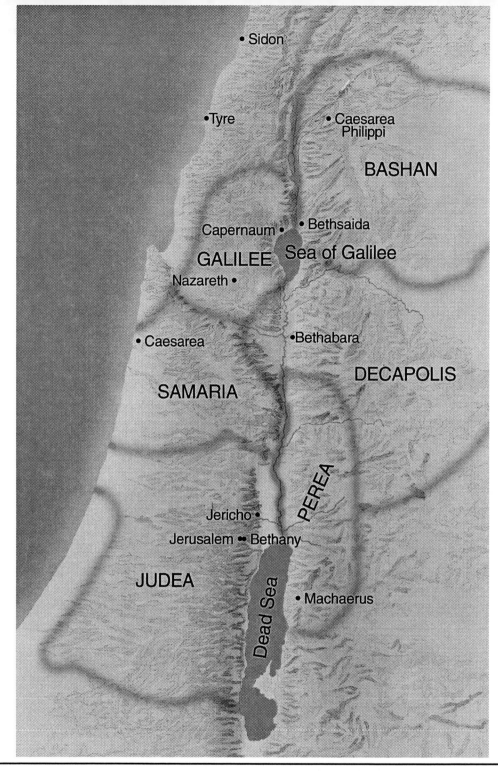

high standard will encourage many students to excel. Provide a "safety net" in the form of extra credit points for those who struggle.

## Bibliography

Included in the Appendix is a bibliography of works consulted in the preparation of this book. The teacher should consider obtaining one or more of these volumes as a general resource for the course. The Student Text of *That I May Know Him* generally does not discuss original language issues, multiple interpretations, or other highly technical matters. The Teacher's Edition does contain more advanced explanations in the margins. Some students may be capable of handling more detailed material. The commentaries may provide the teacher with valuable information for the students.

Finally, teaching is much more than disseminating facts about an academic subject. For the believer, it is modeling and proclaiming a lifestyle that should be pleasing to God. Teens need to see adults who know Jesus Christ personally. Your influence on the next generation of adults and Christian leaders can be enormous. Let Christ and the Word of God forever be your guide and encouragement.

"Take heed unto thyself, and unto the doctrine; continue in them: for in doing this thou shalt both save thyself, and them that hear thee" (I Timothy 4:16).

# The Beginning of the Gospel

**1**

In just two minutes, the bell would ring, signaling the start of the final driver's education class for the year. The state licensing agency opened at 9 A.M. the next day, and Frank Carlson dreamed of being the very first one in line. That is, if Mr. Johnson, the hardest teacher in school, gave him a passing grade. It all depended on the score of the final project, a paper on driver safety. That topic was obviously very important to Mr. Johnson. Each class had started with a short lecture on safety. Each class had ended with an exhortation to be responsible drivers.

Frank shuddered as the bell sounded and a nervous stillness descended over the room. Everyone saw the graded projects in the teacher's hand.

"Class, most of you will soon join the ranks of automobile drivers in our state. The projects were very fine and it will be a great pleasure for me to give many passing grades."

As Mr. Johnson handed back each graded project, he asked the student receiving the paper to state one rule of driver safety. The student glanced at the grade on his paper and then stated a principle. The instructor then reviewed that particular principle before handing back the next paper. The tension in the class rose as students took more of the basic rules. The last person might not have any rules left. Frank's face turned red as the teacher came toward his desk with only one paper in his hand. Kelly Brown had just used his idea and his mind was blank! The grade was a B+!

Frank said nervously, "Mr. Johnson, my father tells me that my actions speak louder than my words and . . . "

## Goals

Students should

1. Consider the relationship between word and action.
2. Know John Mark's background.
3. Understand various names of Christ.
4. Recognize when people's words and actions are not consistent.

## Objectives

Students should be able to

1. State the purpose of Mark's Gospel.
2. Explain how God prepared Mark to write a gospel.
3. Identify key events in Mark's life.
4. Explain the significance of Christ's names and titles.
5. State reasons that Mark gives for Christ's coming to earth.

## Scripture Readings

(Potential assignments at the discretion of the instructor)

1. Mark 1-8
2. Acts 12, 13
3. Isaiah 61

## Memory Verses

(Potential assignments at the discretion of the instructor)

1. Mark 1:1
2. Mark 2:17
3. Mark 10:45

1

## Lecture Overview

### Introduction

1. Personal evaluations are based on actions, not on grades.
2. Personal evaluations are based on your words and your actions.
3. Jesus Christ was a man of mighty words and actions.

### John Mark

1. Mark wrote to the Roman world.
2. Mark saw much of Christianity's early history.
3. Mark's Gospel was well known to the early church fathers.

### Who Is Jesus Christ?

1. Jesus
2. Christ
3. Son of Man

### Why Did Christ Come?

1. To minister
2. To die for sinners

### Our Task

1. To understand Christ's person
2. To allow Christ to change us

## Lesson Plans

(Potential activities at the discretion of the instructor)

**Day 1** The Point Is . . . overhead, Introduction to the study, The Structure of the New Testament overhead

Homework: Read Chapter 1 in Student Text

**Day 2** Chapter lecture

**Day 3** Class reading of Mark, Christ's Old Testament Foundations overhead

**Day 4** The Names of Christ overhead

**Day 5** Chapter Content exercise

## Thoughts for the Teacher

1. The first lesson must start with great enthusiasm lest the students view the entire study as "just another Bible lesson."

2. The first chapter deals with background information that is vital to the lessons that follow. Survey the entire module before teaching the first chapter.

3. Many of the exercises and activities are designed to familiarize the student with the text of Mark. Encourage the students to go beyond their current knowledge of the Bible and to know Christ better.

## Scripture verses on the importance of proper action:

Ecclesiastes 9:10
Matthew 7:21-23
Matthew 12:50
Luke 6:46-49
Romans 2:13
James 1:22

See Romans 7 for Paul's struggle with doing right.

The class broke into hushed laughter as Mr. Johnson stopped Frank midsentence and gave him a thumbs up.

"We studied many rules, laws, and driving tips this semester. Now, the best thing you can do is follow Frank's advice. Your grade means almost nothing. Your actions on the road will speak to everyone about your training and your ability. People will not care about your A or B in this class with me. They will want to see a safe and courteous driver."

My parents told me many times that my actions would speak louder than my words. I got tired of hearing it. As the years pass, I more fully understand their admonitions to me. Talk is free. Action shows character and conviction. I want my friends to be people who back up their words with vigorous action. Tell me, yes; but show me too!

We will study together a man of great deeds as described by another man who valued action more than dialogue. Jesus Christ was the greatest teacher in the world. His eloquent simplicity communicated God's truth both to the scholar and to the child. Some people fail to see that His actions spoke just as mightily as His words. He spoke the truth. He lived the truth.

Most of us know people in church or in school that talk like Christians but don't live like Christians. We know from the Bible that a Christian's walk should match his talk.

The chasm between people's knowledge of what is right and their actions can be wide. Perhaps we see the same chasm in ourselves. It can be very uncomfortable. May I suggest that the problem may be a lack of real understanding about Jesus Christ? The apostle Paul shows us the bridge over this chasm when he declares the desire of his heart, "That I may know him" (Phil. 3:10). We will seek to see and to understand Jesus Christ through this study. Only then will our speech and our actions truly please God.

2

## Overhead: The Point Is . . .

Show each quote on the The Point Is . . . overhead in the Appendix (p. 135) and ask the students to state the meaning in different words. Channel the discussion toward the importance of action. One's actions either confirm or deny his words. Explain that all great men value action as well as words.

## Overhead: Structure of the New Testament

The purpose of The Structure of the New Testament overhead (Appendix, p. 136) is to review the structure of the NT for more experienced students and to show Mark's place in the overall message of the NT. Ask the students to identify the names of the Epistles. Emphasize that the histories establish the facts about Christ and the church. The Epistles relate the doctrinal and practical issues of the Christian life.

Believers must know the facts about Christ before they can live holy lives.

## John Mark

Before looking at the Lord Jesus Christ, we need to spend some time examining how the message of Christ is transmitted to us today. If you and I cannot speak face to face, we are very comfortable talking to one another on the telephone or perhaps through e-mail. Obviously, our modern conveniences were not available two thousand years ago.

God simply used the life and writings of John Mark, an ordinary man, to communicate to us the great message of eternal life in Christ. Mark wrote his Gospel for the benefit of the ancient Roman people.

These people revolted against the Greeks' love of philosophy and talk. They wanted action. Mark simply told them about the deeds of Jesus. He also helped them to understand His words. A main purpose of this course is to give you the skills needed to see and to apply the deeds and words of Christ.

3

Surnames were fairly common in Bible times. A surname could indicate a personal trait, an honorary title, or a future event. It might also allow a person to have a common name in a foreign culture, which seems to be the case with John Mark. The following references contain examples of surnames in the Bible.

Matthew 10:3
Mark 3:16, 17
Luke 22:3
Acts 1:23
Acts 4:36
Acts 12:12
Acts 15:22

---

### Overhead: The Four Gospels

The Four Gospels overhead (Appendix, p. 137) will encourage the students to understand that the four Gospels were written to different audiences and have different purposes. Many reference Bibles, Bible dictionaries, and commentaries will expand upon the similarities and differences in the Gospels.

### Exercise: The Roman World

**Goal:** To expose the students to the achievements and people of the Roman world.

**Procedure:** Have students work on this exercise in teams of two or three. Assign each group a particular facet of Roman culture. The group can use the Internet, the school library, textbooks, etc., to obtain the required information. Each student must report two specific facts about the Roman world.

When doing the exercise as an in-class project, set a time limit for the research. Twenty minutes works well if the research resources are readily available. This exercise can also be used for homework or for extra credit.

### Overhead: Christ's Old Testament Foundations

The Christ's Old Testament Foundations overhead (Appendix, p. 138) will help the students to see that God planned the life and work of Christ.

## Roman Facts

Historians regard the Roman civilization as one of the world's greatest. Consider the following facts:

Time: Centralized Roman power extended from 509 B.C. to A.D. 410. The Roman government in the East lasted until about A.D. 1400. Most modern governments are still infants compared to Rome!

Conquest: Rome conquered significant portions of the known world including parts of Europe, Africa, and Asia. Great armies would defeat a nation and then stay indefinitely to govern for Rome.

Language: The official language of the Roman Empire was Latin. In fact, the Gospel of Mark contains more Latin words than any other New Testament book. Spanish, Italian, and French are direct descendants of Latin. Many of our legal and scientific terms come from Latin words.

Architecture: The Romans built massive structures, many of which still exist today. Tourists often view the Roman Coliseum that was used for fights between gladiators and could even be flooded for naval battles. You can also still see Roman aqueducts that carried water over valleys to large cities.

Law: In 451 B.C. the Romans wrote down the basic precepts of law for society. The law allowed a landowner to cut down part of a tree that hung over his property. A person stealing another man's crops could be put to death. Justinian edited laws from the history of Rome and created what we know today as the Justinian Code. This document is the model for most legal systems of continental Europe.

4

Mark's Gospel records the fulfillment of the plan. The students, working individually or in groups, could look up the verses and report the specific teachings about Christ. Consider drawing the "wall" on the board and having the students write each verse's teaching on a "block."

Let's examine some of the facts of Mark's life. His full name, John Mark, reflected the cultural and ethnic diversity of the Roman world. *John* comes from a Hebrew word meaning "Jehovah has graciously given." *Mark,* on the other hand, was a very common Latin name.

Acts 12:12 indicates that Mark's mother lived in Jerusalem in a house large enough for a meeting of the apostles and the believers. They possibly used her house as a church. Living in Jerusalem may have given Mark the opportunity to see and to hear Jesus for himself. Many Bible scholars believe that Mark mentioned himself in his Gospel.

Mark, *by Guido Reni, Bob Jones University Collection*

> And they all forsook him, and fled. And there followed
> him a certain young man, having a linen cloth cast about
> his naked body; and the young men laid hold on him:
> And he left the linen cloth, and fled from them naked
> (Mark 14:50-52).

None of the other Gospels mention this seemingly minor incident. Confusion and betrayal surrounded Christ at His arrest.

## Using Strong's Concordance

TEXT
TOOLS

A concordance is a book that lists the chapter and verse locations of particular words used in the Bible. Some reference Bibles may also contain a short concordance. By looking up the words *Mark* and *Marcus,* we can find many references to the author of the second Gospel. Many students and scholars believe that the concordance is the most useful of all the Bible study tools. You will have many opportunities to use one in this course.

Could it be that Mark turns his focus from Christ to himself for just a moment to tell us that he was present at this terrible event?

We may assume that Mark saw many of the events in the early chapters of Acts since he lived in Jerusalem and had a close relationship with the apostles. Peter calls Mark "my son" which indicates that Peter had led the young man to saving faith in Christ (I Pet. 5:13). Since Mark's father is not mentioned, we may assume that he was dead at this time. Barnabas and Saul took Mark to the vibrant church in Antioch (Acts 12:25). When the Lord called these two men to preach the gospel in the regions beyond, they took

## The Greek Alphabet

Latin was the language of law and politics, but Greek was the common language of the people. Mark wrote in Koine Greek so that the average person anywhere in the Roman world could learn about Jesus. You are very familiar with some different forms of English letters—capital and lower case. In Greek, an uncial was the form of a letter used when writing quickly was important. Most business contracts and personal correspondence used uncials. How many Greek letters do you recognize in the picture of Mark's Gospel on the next page?

| name | capital | lower | uncial | name | capital | lower | uncial |
|---|---|---|---|---|---|---|---|
| Alpha | A | α | ⅄ | Nu | N | ν | Ͷ |
| Beta | B | β | Ᏸ | Xi | Ξ | ξ | ⟨ |
| Gamma | Γ | γ | Γ | Omicron | O | o | O |
| Delta | Δ | δ | Δ | Pi | Π | π | ⊓ |
| Epsilon | E | ε | Є | Rho | P | ρ | Ρ |
| Zeta | Z | ζ | Ζ | Sigma | Σ | σ | C |
| Eta | H | η | Η | Tau | T | τ | Τ |
| Theta | Θ | θ | Θ | Upsilon | Y | υ | Υ |
| Iota | I | ι | Ι | Phi | Φ | φ | Φ |
| Kappa | K | κ | Κ | Chi | X | χ | ✕ |
| Lambda | Λ | λ | ⅄ | Psi | Ψ | ψ | ✝ |
| Mu | M | μ | Ϻ | Omega | Ω | ω | ⱳ |

Mark as a helper (Acts 13:5). After the incident with Elymas the sorcerer, Mark returned to his home in Jerusalem perhaps due to his youth or out of fear (Acts 13:13). Conceivably, he came back under the influence of Peter's ministry in Jerusalem. Later, Barnabas and Paul went their separate ways because Barnabas wanted to take Mark on their next trip and Paul did not (Acts 15:37-39).

Peter and Paul both mention in their letters that Mark was present with them in various locations. Paul's references to Mark (Col. 4:10; Philem. 24; II Tim. 4:11) indicate that he traveled with the apostle and that he performed valuable services in the ministry.

We may conclude that Paul's estimate of Mark's character had improved over time. Peter tells us that Mark was with him in "Babylon" (I Pet. 5:13). Scholars debate whether this was the actual city named Babylon or a figure of speech for Rome. In either case, the implication is that Mark was well known to the churches and that he was working with Peter.

Mark's association with the apostles allowed him to hear great preaching about Christ, to see the power of God in lives, and to watch as these men wrote instructional letters to the churches. We would not classify Mark as one of the great men of the Bible like Peter or Paul. However, God put Mark in a very strategic location to observe and to digest more of Christianity's development than perhaps any other person. God was simply preparing Mark to write the story of Jesus Christ for our benefit!

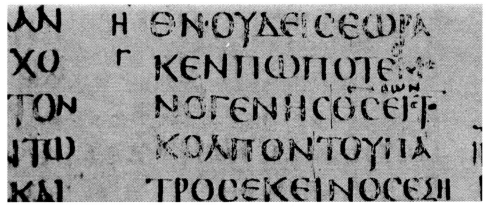

7

## *E*arly References to Mark's Gospel

A quick reading of the Gospel of Mark reveals that many of the events occurred outside Jerusalem. How is it that Mark could write about Christ's experiences prior to His arrival in Jerusalem where Mark lived?

We know from the verses above that Mark spent much time with Peter who was with Jesus during most of His public ministry. Peter undoubtedly told the story of Christ time and time again as he traveled and as people came to him. It makes sense then that Mark may have recorded the preaching of Peter about the life of Christ.

God raised up a group of men that we know as the "church fathers" following the times of the apostles. We have various

### The Canon of Scripture

*Canon* reminds us of a great military weapon used to shoot explosives at the enemy! In biblical studies, the word refers to a standard of measurement, like a yardstick or a ruler. During the time of the apostles and in the years following, many books and letters circulated among believers. Some of these writings were obviously defective or of inferior quality. The Christians agreed that the following "measurements" showed which writings were authoritative and should be included in the New Testament.

1. The book must be written by an apostle or someone closely associated with an apostle.
2. The book must agree with the teaching of the rest of Scripture.
3. The book must be universally accepted by diverse parts of the church.
4. The book must show evidences of being inspired by the Holy Spirit.

God used the early Christians to compile the proper writings into the New Testament. Over the centuries, God used men to copy the books and to translate them into the languages of the world. We may have absolute confidence that our English Bible is God's Word to us.

writings from these men about the apostles and about early church history. These leaders tell us that Mark's Gospel contains the teachings of Peter. Eusebius quotes Papias (about A.D. 125 in Asia Minor) as saying,

> Mark, having become the interpreter of Peter, wrote accurately what he remembered of the things said or done by Christ, but not in order. For he took thought for one thing not to omit any of the things he had heard nor to falsify anything in them.

Eusebius also quotes Irenaeus from about A.D. 175 in Gaul:

> But after the departure of these (Peter and Paul), Mark, the disciple and interpreter of Peter, even he has delivered to us in writing the things which were preached by Peter.

Scholars love to examine even the smallest details of biblical history. The majority, both ancient and modern, confirm that Mark's Gospel is an accurate record of the teachings and actions of Christ. We can have absolute confidence in God's communication to us. Our job is to learn how to listen to it.

## Who Is Jesus Christ?

Peter was a decisive man who generally got right to the point. Mark seems to follow his teacher's style by giving us a brief and yet powerful introduction to Jesus: "The beginning of the gospel of Jesus Christ, the Son of God" (Mark 1:1).

Mark's view of the person and work of Christ is the central focus of the entire book. Our understanding of Jesus' actions and teachings depends upon our ability to see the truths expressed in the very first verse of the book.

Eusebius (A.D. 260-339), Bishop of Caesarea, wrote *Ecclesiastical History,* which detailed the events of the church from the apostles through the time of Constantine. Much of our current knowledge of early church history is due to Eusebius's efforts and writing.

Papias, Bishop of Hierapolis, was a disciple of John the Apostle.

Irenaeus (A.D. 120-200) defended Christianity against the Gnostic heresy and is credited with helping to formulate the canon of Scripture.

## Worksheet: Names of Christ

Duplicate the Names of Christ worksheet (Appendix, p. 139-40) and give one to each student. Emphasize that names and titles often indicate a person's character or rank. Students should look up the verses and fill out the worksheet. Instruct the students to write a brief paragraph on the back of the sheet about the importance of one of the names. Consider giving extra credit for the paragraph.

(Based on "The Theology of Mark" by Stewart Custer, *Biblical Viewpoint,* November 1977.)

The names of Christ in the NT occur at the following frequencies:

**Jesus (only)**

| | |
|---|---|
| Mark | 95 |
| Gospels | 613 |
| Entire NT | 707 |

**Christ (only)**

| | |
|---|---|
| Mark | 8 |
| Gospels | 48 |
| Entire NT | 276 |

**Jesus Christ**

| | |
|---|---|
| Mark | 1 |
| Gospels | 24 |
| Entire NT | 510 |

**Son of Man**

| | |
|---|---|
| Mark | 15 |
| Gospels | 84 |
| Entire NT | 86 |

We may conclude that *Jesus* was the personal name of the Messiah used in the Gospels. Also, the term *Christ* was not commonly applied to the *Jesus* until after the Resurrection. The four Gospels record the revelation of Jesus as the Christ to the disciples and to the world. "Son of man" is used by Jesus to refer to Himself more than any other name. The term points to both Christ's humility and His incarnation.

First, let's examine the person of Christ through His names and titles. Keep in mind that names in the ancient world carried much more meaning than names do today. *Jesus* is the Greek form of the common Jewish name meaning "Jehovah saves." It is equivalent to the Hebrew name *Joshua*. God first promised a deliverer from sin in Genesis 3:15 and then repeated the promise in various ways and at different times. The story of the Old Testament revolves around the hopes and preparations for the one who would deliver God's people from their sins. Near the time of Jesus' birth, the angel of the Lord spoke to Joseph saying,

Joseph, thou son of David, fear not to take unto thee Mary thy wife: for that which is conceived in her is of the Holy Ghost. And she shall bring forth a son, and thou shalt call his name Jesus: for he shall save his people from their sins (Matt. 1:20, 21).

The name *Jesus* identifies the subject of Mark's Gospel with God's intention to save His people. It also shows us that Jesus was fully human. He had a human body that required food and rest. Jesus often called Himself the "Son of man" which reinforced His humanity to the hearers. He was born just like any other man except that He was conceived by the Holy Spirit. As a man, Jesus understood the frailties of humanity and exercised great compassion on those in need. Since the Holy Spirit conceived Jesus in Mary's womb, Jesus did not possess a sin nature. He did not sin against God as you and I are so prone to do. In every respect, Jesus was the perfect man.

The word *christ* is not a name, but is rather a title for the Jewish messiah. Both the Greek term *christ* and the Hebrew term *messiah* mean "anointed one." The Old Testament records the practice of pouring oil on the heads of men specifically set apart for three types of divine service.

Samuel anointed Saul and David as kings of Israel (I Sam. 9:16; 16:13). Moses anointed Aaron as the high priest (Exod. 29:7). Elijah anointed Elisha as a prophet (I Kings 19:16). The Israelites clearly looked for an anointed leader that would deliver them from bondage.

> The Spirit of the Lord God is upon me; because the Lord hath **anointed** me to preach good tidings unto the meek; he hath sent me to bind up the brokenhearted, to proclaim liberty to the captives, and the opening of the prison to them that are bound; to proclaim the acceptable year of the Lord, and the day of vengeance of our God; to comfort all that mourn; to appoint unto them that mourn in Zion, to give unto them beauty for ashes, the oil of joy for mourning, the garment of praise for the spirit of heaviness; that they might be called trees of righteousness, the planting of the Lord, that he might be glorified (Isa. 61:1-3).

Jesus performed the duties of a prophet by teaching God's truth to all men. He acted as a priest by sacrificing Himself to reconcile sinners to God. Believers follow Him as their king. One day, Jesus will be King over all mankind. Jesus was the fulfillment of the Jewish expectation for a messiah. John the Baptist announced His coming to the nation (John 1:29-37). A few of Jesus' disciples quickly recognized Him as the Messiah (John 1:43-51). Others took much longer. Only after the Resurrection did most of the disciples truly understand Jesus' position. Many of the Jewish leaders rejected Him altogether. Mark tells us plainly who Jesus is from the very beginning of his book. We can then watch and learn from Jesus as He reveals Himself to mankind.

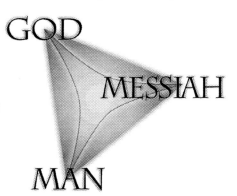

GOD

MESSIAH

MAN

Isaiah uses Hebrew parallelism to express God's authorization of Christ's ministry in verse 1.

The Lord anointed me to preach . . .

He (the Lord) sent me to bind up . . .

The infinitives show the purposes of Christ's ministry. Reading any of the Gospels looking for the fulfillment of these purposes provides significant insight into the ministry of Christ.

**Prophet** a person who speaks for God

Deuteronomy 18:18
Matthew 21:11, 46
John 4:19; 6:14
Hebrews 1:1, 2

**Priest** a person who intercedes between God and man. Christ's priesthood is a major theme in the book of Hebrews.

Hebrews 2:17; 4:14, 15; 5:5; 6:20; 7:26; 8:1

**King** a person who rules under God's authority

Isaiah 9:7
Jeremiah 23:5
Mark 15:2, 26
John 1:49
Revelation 1:5; 19:16

**PRINCIPLES APPLIED**

## What Is Sin?

Choose the best answer.

A. Sin is simply a mistake—writing the number 5 on a math test instead of 3.

B. Sin is an accident—tripping over a baseball bat in your yard.

C. Sin is a missed opportunity—not being able to go to the mountains on the weekend.

D. Sin is the poor appearance of an object—my brother's wrecked car.

E. Sin is breaking the law of God—stealing or lying.

People often use the word *sin* in a casual manner to refer to something accidental or unfortunate. According to the Bible, sin is a very serious issue. What are the implications of man's sin according to the following verses?

Whosoever committeth sin transgresseth also the law: for sin is the transgression of the law (I John 3:4).

For all have sinned, and come short of the glory of God (Rom. 3:23).

For the wages of sin is death; but the gift of God is eternal life through Jesus Christ our Lord (Rom. 6:23).

Mark also tells us that Jesus was the "Son of God." Jewish leaders of the day well understood that the Messiah would be God's Son, and therefore He would be equal to God (Matt. 26:63).

The grammar of the original language indicates that Mark is focusing on Jesus' character or quality as deity. While studying Mark's Gospel together, we will see that only God could do many of the things that Jesus did. His Resurrection from the dead and His ascension into heaven forever sealed this truth in the disciples' minds.

See Romans 1:4 and Ephesians 1:19-23.

# Why Did Jesus Come?

Mark begins his story with an exalted and honoring proclamation about the identity of Jesus. If we understand who He is, then logically we need to investigate why He came to earth and what He did while here. Jesus Himself reveals the answers to us:

> And he said unto them, Let us go into the next towns, that I may preach there also: for therefore came I forth (Mark 1:38).

> When Jesus heard it, he saith unto them, They that are whole have no need of the physician, but they that are sick: I came not to call the righteous, but sinners to repentance (Mark 2:17).

> For even the Son of man came not to be ministered unto, but to minister, and to give his life a ransom for many (Mark 10:45).

Mankind honors great political leaders, sports stars, and military heroes by meeting their every need and whim. Higher rank or accomplishment brings ever-increasing money, fame, and respect.

Those attaining high achievement expect "royal" treatment. Jesus Christ, the greatest man ever, walked a different path. Notice in the verses above that Jesus' ministry focused on the common people in the villages, on the sick, and on sinners. He came to teach, to heal, and to meet the needs of hurting men. His greatest act was His death in place of sinners. God justly sentenced man to death for breaking the law and for turning from righteousness. Jesus interceded by dying in man's place so

13

Most Bible translations strive for readability. Understanding the text must be the focus of Bible study. Simple grammatical analysis, similar to sentence diagramming, can help the students extract the meaning of a passage. Limit the exercise to a single clause and then look for the subject, main verb, and object. Construct a simple sentence using the parts. In this case, each example shows a reason that Jesus came to earth.

### Examples

Mark 1:38—Jesus came to preach.

Mark 2:17—Jesus came to call sinners to repentance.

Mark 10:45—Jesus came to minister and to give His life.

See the following verses on Jesus' control of His death: John 10:15, 17, 18; 15:13.

that man could be free from sin. In fact, the word *give* implies that Jesus was in full control of His situation and did not lose His life as a criminal or by accident. He purposed to die for man. Mark will show us the purposes and heart of Christ in every chapter.

Remember that Mark starts his Gospel with "the beginning of the gospel of Jesus Christ." The word *gospel* means "good news." A beginning implies a continuation. Mark wrote possibly thirty years after the time of Christ. The proclamation of sins forgiven was still good news to all. It should be the same for us today.

## Our Task

Let's briefly review some facts that Mark presents to us. Jesus Christ is fully human and fully divine. As a man, He can sympathize with our weaknesses and our failures. As God, He is able to show us the truth and to relieve our problems. We cannot understand how Jesus could be both God and man, but it is the clear teaching of the Bible. The great prophet Isaiah proclaimed, "Therefore the Lord himself shall give you a sign; Behold, a virgin shall conceive, and bear a son, and shall call his name Immanuel" (Isa. 7:14). The Gospel of Matthew tells us that *Emmanuel* means, "God with us" (Matt. 1:23). Jesus is the bridge between God and man, and also between our failures and the wonderful life that God wants us to have.

14

### Exercise: Chapter Content

**Goal:** To become familiar with the major events in Mark.

**Procedure:** Divide the class into groups of two or three students. Assign each group either Mark 1-8 or Mark 9-16. More than one group may work on the same chapters. Instruct the students to quickly read each chapter and, as a group, decide what the main event is. Also have them list one or two secondary events. Write numbers 1-16, corresponding to the chapters in Mark, across the top of the board. Each group then writes on the board what the group considers to be the primary and secondary events for the particular chapter. As groups disagree about the primary event, encourage a discussion about the different choices.

This exercise could be assigned as homework or could span portions of two class periods.

**14**

As we study the Gospel of Mark, let's be alert to Jesus' humanity. Let's look for His words and actions as God. Christ continually interacted with various people. Some are much like you and me. Jesus completely transformed those that chose to believe and to follow Him. Mark started off as a weak young man who deserted his friends. He ended up as a choice instrument in the hand of God. Peter began as an impetuous fisherman. Jesus molded him into a servant who literally changed the entire world. We can know the same Jesus and experience the same change as Peter and Mark.

15

## Class Discussion: Failures and Successes

Invite a pastor, principal, missionary, or another Christian leader to class to talk about people they know who failed or succeeded. Ask the speaker to emphasize faith and obedience to Christ as the key to spiritual growth and success. Allow the students to ask questions and make observations.

# Review Questions

1. Who called Mark "my son"?

    **Peter**

2. What city did Mark live in?

    **Jerusalem**

3. Who refused to take Mark on a mission trip?

    **Paul**

4. What does the name "Jesus" mean?

    **Jehovah saves**

5. Whose teaching about Jesus did Mark record?

    **Peter's**

6. What is the Greek word that means "messiah"?

    **Christ**

7. Who announced Jesus' coming to the Jewish nation?

    **John the Baptist**

8. What type of book lists chapter and verse locations for words used in the Bible?

    **Concordance**

9. What does the term *gospel* mean?

    **Good news**

10. To whom did Mark write his Gospel?

    **The ancient Roman people**

11. Why did Mark have two names?

   *The two names reflected the different cultures that are associated with Mark. John is a Jewish name while Mark is Roman.*

12. How could Mark write about Jesus when he did not have first-hand knowledge about all of Jesus' life?

   *Mark recorded the teaching and preaching of Peter, who was with Jesus from the beginning.*

13. According to the verses in this chapter, what was the function of the Holy Spirit in Jesus' life?

   *The Holy Spirit conceived the body of Jesus in Mary and empowered Jesus' ministry.*

14. Why did Jesus come to earth?

*Jesus came to earth to minister to people and to die for sinners.*

15. How did Mark imitate his teachers?

*Mark imitated Peter and Paul by writing about Jesus and by following their example of ministry to others.*

# Christ and the Multitudes

2

"Load up! Let's move out!" rang through the house. Dad signaled the start of another car trip. Jared and Tessa moved with more speed than usual as they gathered up the last of the supplies and food. This time, the family was going on vacation for ten days to a cabin in a national park.

Dad looked forward to the trout fishing. Mom simply wanted to rest and maybe work on a cross-stitch project. Jared and Tessa had other plans.

"Dad, I have a question." Jared spoke tentatively about two hours into the trip.

"Let me guess, you need to stop at a rest area," Mom responded while Dad changed lanes on the highway.

Jared and Tessa shook their heads.

Dad turned down the CD player and cast a puzzled glance through the rearview mirror at Jared.

Jared started, "You know that Tessa and I get bored at the cabin after a couple of days. We thought about hiking to that little village to the east of the park for a day. It's only three miles and we could be back by supper."

Mom and Dad looked at each other cautiously.

Tessa spoke up this time, "We want to watch the man who makes the chocolate candies for our school fundraisers. He told us to visit his shop the next time we came to the cabin. Besides,

## Goals

Students should

1. Recognize Jesus' credentials as a teacher.
2. Understand the concept of the kingdom of God.
3. Understand the nature of parables.
4. Consider their personal response to Christ's teaching.
5. Evaluate their spiritual receptiveness and progress.

## Objectives

Students will be able to

1. Explain why people were attracted to Jesus.
2. Explain why Jesus traveled to the people.
3. Identify important facets of the kingdom.
4. State how to enter God's kingdom.

### Scripture Readings

1. Mark 9-16
2. Isaiah 9
3. John 3

### Memory Verses

1. Mark 1:14,15
2. Mark 3:35

## Lecture Overview

### The Master Teacher

1. Common people listened eagerly to Christ.
2. Christ was both God and man.
3. Christ can solve the sin problem of ordinary people.

### The Kingdom of God

1. The nature of a kingdom
2. Christ is the King.
3. Repentance and faith are needed to enter the kingdom.

### The Kingdom in Parables

1. The nature of a parable
2. Parable of the Soils
3. Parable of the Growing Seed
4. Parable of the Mustard Seed

### The Kingdom for Common People

1. Rejecting the kingdom
2. Entering the kingdom

## Lesson Plans

**Day 1** Class reading of Mark

Homework: Read Student Text Chapter 2

**Day 2** Christ the Master Teacher lecture, Teachings of Christ in Mark worksheet

**Day 3** The Kingdom of God lecture, Roman Domination of Palestine overhead, Word Meanings exercise

**Day 4** Parables lecture, Write a Parable exercise

**Day 5** What's Your Soil Type? exercise, Seed Potentials exercise

## Thoughts for the Teacher

1. Just as Mark is a book of action, so the teaching session should be active and vibrant.

2. Chapter 2 deals with Christ's general ministry to the multitudes. His words are intended to draw men closer to Himself for additional training. Many students may understand the gospel for the first time. Always be willing and prepared to deal privately with any student who desires to know more.

3. More than five days may be required to cover all the materials in this chapter. Adapt the lesson plans to the needs of the students and to the allocated time. In most cases, covering one concept well is better than poorly skimming over too much material.

4. The verses in the margins may be used to supplement personal study or classroom exercises.

as soon as school starts in the fall, the teachers assign a report on life in small towns. I need all the information that I can get."

Dad responded in an unusual way, "Did the two of you realize that small towns attracted Jesus too?"

This time, Jared and Tessa looked at each other.

"I will approve the trip with two conditions," Dad continued. "You must find out what Jesus did in the villages of His day and then imitate Him in at least one way."

"What's the other condition?" Tessa asked.

"Be back before supper!"

Jared and Tessa kept busy learning about Jesus in the Gospels and then had a great day in the village. They decided to imitate Jesus by giving out the small New Testaments that Dad kept in the van. The vacation was fantastic!

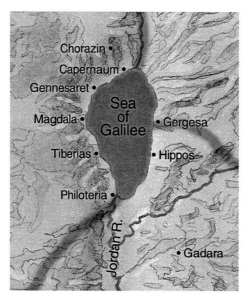

## *T*he Master Teacher

Jared and Tessa's father was correct in his statement that Jesus spent much time in the villages and small towns of Israel. Mark shows us that Jesus constantly traveled from one place to the next.

> And he said unto them, Let us go into the next towns, that I may preach there also: for therefore came I forth. And he preached in their synagogues throughout all Galilee, and cast out devils (Mark 1:38, 39).

20

### Exercise: Read the Text

Several ideas for reading the text of Mark as a class appear in the Appendix (p. 134). Select the most appropriate method for the class. Reading and comprehending the text of Mark should be the main priority for at least one day per week and for the course as a whole.

Great multitudes often gathered to see and hear Jesus. Sometimes the crowd was so huge that Jesus could not even eat! Mark 12:37 tells us that "the common people heard him gladly." What attracted Jesus to the small cities and villages? What attracted the multitudes of Israel to Him? Much of this book will seek to answer those questions.

Let's focus first of all on the fact that Jesus was a master teacher. We believe that He was the greatest teacher ever! Keep in mind that Jesus is God's Son, and therefore He is God. This gives Jesus a perspective on truth and reality that sinful humans do not have. He could explain God's view on every issue of life. Jesus is also a man and as a man, He understands the rigors and challenges of living for God on earth. Putting His two natures together means that He could teach God's truth in human terms so everyone could understand.

Teaching is hard work. Ask any of your instructors! Often after teaching the multitude, Jesus would have a private session for the disciples. We will study some of those times in another chapter. Also, teachers in the ancient world normally stayed in one place and the students came to them. Jesus traveled from village to village so that everyone could hear the message from God. It's easy to understand why He needed rest.

I have traveled to many places both in this country and around the world. Talking to people, eating various types of food, listening to strange languages, and watching many activities leads me to a simple conclusion: people are basically the same. They have similar desires, hopes, and difficulties. The main problem throughout history is sin, which results in a broken relationship to God. Jesus knew the problem well. He taught the people of His day about knowing God personally. His teachings are as fresh today as they were two thousand years ago. Let's look at some of Jesus' words so that our relationship to God might flourish.

21

See Mark 1:38; 6:6, 36, 56; and 8:27 for Jesus' routine of going into towns and villages.

See the following verses about Christ and the multitude:

Mark 2:13; 3:7-9, 20, 32; 4:1, 36; 5:31; 7:33; 8:1, 2; 9:14, 17.

Mark records twelve times that Jesus was called "teacher." Each time, the English word *master* is translated from the Greek word *didaskalos.* See Mark 4:38; 5:35; 9:17, 38; 10:17, 20, 35; 12:14, 19, 32; 13:1; 14:14.

*Rabbi,* the Jewish term denoting "master" or "teacher," occurs in Mark 9:5; 11:21; and 14:45.

*Rabbouni,* "my master," occurs in Mark 10:51.

Continually stress the fact that Jesus taught well because He is both God and man. Sinful man must forsake his own flawed views of reality and accept the views of God as communicated by Christ.

## Different Cultures

Invite a person familiar with a foreign culture to talk to the class about the differences and the similarities of people in other cultures. Instruct the presenter several days before class about the goals for the session. Ask him to emphasize the problems of sin common to both cultures. Some parents and missionaries with the right experience make good candidates for the presentation.

## Worksheet: Teachings of Christ in Mark

**Goals:** Survey additional teachings of Christ in Mark. Develop theme recognition skills.

**Procedure:** Duplicate the Teachings of Christ in Mark worksheet in the Appendix (pp. 141-42). Students may work individually or in pairs. Have them complete any unfinished items for homework. People may differ regarding the statement of the theme.

You may need to judge the validity of the students' answers. The Appendix also contains an answer key. Allow two or more students to read their themes for the same passage. Use each passage to discuss the accuracy of the theme and the application of Christ's teaching.

## The Kingdom of God

Jesus started a new phase of His work when He entered Galilee (Mark 1:16) and started preaching a simple but profound message. Notice that Jesus is taking the message directly to the people. Both Mark and Jesus seem to assume that the reader and the hearer would understand the basics of the kingdom. Since we are removed both in time and in culture from their situation, we may need to consider some foundational principles before looking at Jesus' specific teaching.

A kingdom certainly implies a king. It also implies a people or land to rule, and a means by which that rule is carried out. Your younger brother may make a crown and dress up like royalty. He may then proclaim that he is king over the entire country. He has a land to rule but does not have the means to carry out his rule. You will probably consider his actions to be humorous. To the Romans, the concept of a kingdom was no laughing matter. They lived and worked under the authority of the Emperor who had almost absolute power. The Roman armies regularly crushed any threat, or any rumored threat, to their power. They had controlled Palestine for about ninety years when Jesus started preaching. The Romans would not be happy about the kingdom of God.

But for the Jews, the kingdom of God would be good news. They looked for a man to take the throne of David (Isa. 9:7) and then to reestablish the sovereignty of Israel. Their hatred of foreign governments blinded them to the fact that the kingdom of God starts as a personal relationship to Him and that the political phase would come later in time.

Let's examine Jesus' teaching about entering into the kingdom.

> Now after that John was put in prison, Jesus came into Galilee, preaching the gospel of the kingdom of God, And saying, The time is fulfilled, and the kingdom of God is at hand: repent ye, and believe the gospel (Mark 1:14, 15).

John the Baptist preached about the kingdom, and also that a much greater man was about to appear (Mark 1:7, 8). John's public ministry ended when he was imprisoned. It seems logical that the next major event would be the appearance of this great man.

22

---

Encyclopedias, history books, and the Internet contain volumes of good information about the Romans and their activities. The Romans governed through vassal kings from the provinces. Rome granted significant freedom to the kings as long as the kings paid taxes, kept public order, and remained loyal to the empire. Rome sent procurators that answered directly to the emperor to rule in troublesome areas.

The Jews as a whole despised the Romans as foreigners who had imported pagan culture into Palestine. Many rulers, both Roman and native Palestinian, provoked the Jews by insensitive decrees and behavior.

### Roman Domination
See the following passages that relate to the officials cited in the overhead:

Herod the Great—Matthew 2

Note that Herod built the great temple in Jerusalem that is often mentioned in the Gospels.

Archelaus—Matthew 2:22

Herod Antipas—Mark 6:14 ff.; Luke 13:31; 23:7 ff.

Philip the Tetrarch—Luke 3:1; Mark 6:17

Philip built the city Caesarea Philippi, mentioned in Mark 8:27.

### Jewish Hopes for a Kingdom
The disciples' questions to Jesus about a kingdom reflected the thinking of Jewish society during the first century: "Lord, wilt thou at this time restore again the kingdom to Israel?" (Acts 1:6).

---

## Overhead: Roman Domination of Palestine

**Goal:** To acquaint the students with Roman activity in Palestine and with the reasons for Jewish reactions to it.

**Procedure:** See the Roman Domination of Palestine overhead in the Appendix (p. 143). Show one section of the overhead and ask the students to find biblical references to the events or people. A concordance may be required. Be prepared to supplement the students' findings accordingly. As time permits, allow the students to search the library or the Internet for information on Roman activity in Palestine. Use a map to find the various places. Start a discussion on the reasons for Jewish hatred of the Romans. Lead them to understand that the kingdom of God should have been welcome news.

## Life in Galilee

**HISTORICAL LIGHT**

Galilee was well known in the Roman world for fine agricultural products. Most families in the region farmed and raised livestock. Fishing was the main industry in the towns and villages bordering the Sea of Galilee. The region's natural resources supported the largest population in Palestine and perhaps one of the wealthiest.

Nazareth, Jesus' boyhood home, was typical of most villages of the day. A major trade route passed nearby and probably gave the village a steady stream of outside merchants and visitors. Most homes were made of stone or clay bricks. Houses were tightly packed together for mutual security. People dumped their garbage on the few narrow streets. The center of town contained a Jewish synagogue and was the location of the main religious and social event of the week. Ladies went to the local well at least once a day for the family's water. The open-air market contained local produce and household products. Each purchase required an intense price negotiation between buyer and seller. All boys learned a trade and some attended formal Jewish schools. Girls prepared for marriage by gaining the skills needed to manage a household.

They viewed the kingdom of God as a Jewish state in the promised land. Greek and Roman influences only sharpened the desire for a new Jewish political kingdom.

Conservative theologians often disagree about the nature of the kingdom. In the most basic manifestation, it is the rule and dominion of God. In Mark 10:14-27 and 12:34, Jesus stressed that the kingdom could be received by individuals. God reigns over believers today and will reign over the world in the millennial kingdom. Finally, God will rule in the eternal state of heaven. God also currently rules over the affairs of heaven and earth.

Mark and the other New Testament writers teach that the kingdom of God is closely connected to Christ.

See Mark 6:14-29 for the details of John's imprisonment.

23

## Exercise: Word Meanings

**Goal:** To think about significant words that we often hear and take for granted.

**Procedure:** Provide several English dictionaries, concordance dictionaries, theological dictionaries, and/or Internet sites. Instruct the students to find and record the meanings for the words *faith, believe, gospel, repent,* and *kingdom.* Read Mark 1:15 and ask the students to fill in an expanded definition in place of the single words used in the verse. Review the concepts with object lessons, short stories, and personal experiences.

Jesus' first announcement of the kingdom came in Galilee. Many of the Jews would recognize this as the realization of Isaiah 9:1, 2 where the prophet indicates that Galilee would see a great light. Jesus also teaches that the fulfillment of Old Testament promises about the Messiah was very near. The clear implication is that the person making the announcement, Jesus, was none other than the king. All the blessings and benefits of the kingdom would be found in and through Him.

## Foreign Domination of Palestine

Roman history is divided into two great periods. The Roman Republic (509-27 B.C.) saw Rome's expansion throughout much of the known world. The great general Pompey conquered Jerusalem in 63 B.C. and brought Palestine under Roman domination. Decapolis, a league of ten Greek cities built to the east and south of Galilee by Roman officials, provided a base for control and often provoked the Jewish inhabitants. The Roman Empire (27 B.C.–A.D. 476) governed by a long series of emperors. Tiberius (A.D. 14-37), emperor during Christ's life, used a succession of procurators and vassal kings to control the provinces. Pontius Pilate ruled Judea for the emperor through taxation, military operations, and civil courts. He allowed the Jews to have some religious courts and limited civil power.

Herod Antipas ruled Galilee and Perea for Rome during the time of Christ's ministry. He built the city of Tiberias on top of an old cemetery near the western shore of the Sea of Galilee. Most Jews despised this city honoring the Roman emperor.

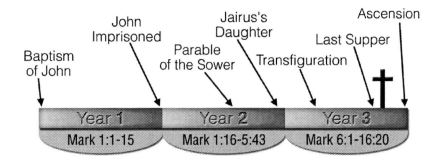

Baptism of John — Year 1 — Mark 1:1-15
John Imprisoned — Parable of the Sower — Jairus's Daughter — Year 2 — Mark 1:16-5:43
Transfiguration — Last Supper — Ascension — Year 3 — Mark 6:1-16:20

If the kingdom of God were a political movement, you would expect Jesus to announce the formation of an army or a government. Instead, he turned the people's attention to the real problem. The word *repent* means "to change the mind" or "to change direction." Jesus preached that man has a sin problem. That sin must be acknowledged and forsaken. He also announced the necessity of faith, or belief in the good news. Abraham, the father of the nation, had believed God in very difficult circumstances. Now the Jews of Galilee must do the same. To enter the kingdom, they must believe in Jesus as their King and turn away from their sins.

The Gospel of Mark records about fourteen occasions when Jesus taught specifically about the kingdom. We will see in the following chapters that His actions confirm His claims as King. The multitudes and religious leaders eventually rejected Jesus and His teachings about the kingdom. They stubbornly held onto their traditions, culture, and religious heritage. Man has not changed much over the centuries. We still prefer to make our own rules for a relationship with God and for our behavior. In a political kingdom, a man is quickly imprisoned and punished for failing to obey the orders of the king. The same is true in spiritual matters. For our own good, we need to enter the kingdom according to God's design.

Faith is much more than a mental acknowledgment of the truth. Faith forms a bond of dependence between the believer and the truth.

See Romans 4:17-22; Hebrews 11; James 2:14-26.

Jesus teaches about the kingdom in the following passages: Mark 1:14 ff.; 4:11, 26, 30; 9:1, 47; 10:14 ff.; 12:34; 14:25.

Many other passages either allude to or have some relationship to the kingdom.

25

## The Kingdom in Parables

Jesus was in the middle of another long, busy day. The scribes had accused Him of having a very wicked association with Satan (Mark 3:22-30). Then some of Jesus' family members had prompted a discussion about the priority of spiritual relationships (Mark 3:31-35). At the close of the day, Jesus took a boat trip to the other side of Galilee and fell asleep during the voyage. A great storm threatened the boat when Jesus simply uttered, "Peace, be still," to calm the sea (Mark 4:39).

Between these events, Jesus taught great multitudes as He sat in a boat and the people sat on the shore. Mark indicates that this was a prolonged session. Many regard this day as the very climax of Jesus' great ministry in Galilee. He used a story-like teaching method known as a parable to relate spiritual truths in ordinary

*The Sea of Galilee*

26

Hiebert designates the events of Matthew 12:22–13:53; Mark 3:19–4:41; and Luke 8:4-25 as "Christ's busy day at Capernaum" (Hiebert, 105).

It is uncertain if this day represented a typical day in Christ's ministry. Mark 4 indicates that the teaching session in the boat lasted for a long time. Mark omits some of the parables, according to 4:33, 34.

Hiebert suggests that a steep bank next to the Sea of Galilee created an ideal amphitheater as the setting for Christ's instruction.

"Here is a strange Teacher; His parables are designed to test, not the intelligence, but the spiritual responsiveness of the hearers. Further, there is a sort of arithmetical progression in things spiritual; to him that already has something, more will be given (Matt. 25:29), and insight into the meaning of one parable will lead to spiritual perception of the meaning of other such parables" (Cole, 88).

### Exercise: Write a Parable

**Goal:** To encourage the students to think about the nature of parables.

**Procedure:** Review the basic nature and format of a Bible parable. Ask the students to write a parable by first selecting the primary truth and then writing an appropriate fictitious story about sports, music, friends, or something else especially applicable to teens. The book of Proverbs will supply many easy-to-understand truths.

Collect the parables for a grade and then select several to read to the class. Ask the class to identify the basic truth in each parable.

## The Jewish Tradition of Parables

TEXT TOOLS

The word *parable* in Greek means "to place beside" and therefore "to compare." Using a ruler, we can determine the length of a candy bar. The candy bar does not change in any way, but we understand its size better when we compare it to the ruler. Jewish teachers often told stories about everyday events to explain truths that otherwise may have been unclear to the listener. Parables are common in Jewish writings and in the Old Testament. Look up the following parables and write the meaning using one sentence.

Judges 9:8-15 _____

II Samuel 12:1-4 _____

Isaiah 5:1-7 _____

_____

events. Some folks would dismiss a parable as just a nice story. To them, the deeper truths were concealed. Parables were intended to make people think about spiritual issues. The more serious listeners might be rewarded with fuller explanations in private or with additional capacity to understand (Mark 4:24, 25). Jesus generally tried to communicate one central truth in each parable. Many of the details exist only to tell the story. The details have minimal spiritual importance. He often ended a parable with, "If any man have ears to hear, let him hear" (Mark 4:23). Let's make sure that our ears are open as Jesus relates three parables about farming that teach us about the kingdom.

27

### Parable of the Soils

Jesus told a story that we might know as the parable of the sower. Some also call it the parable of the soils. A farmer would use a wooden plow pulled by oxen to break up the hard dirt. At the right time, he would walk through the field and throw handfuls of seed onto the prepared ground. The seed grew and prospered depending upon where it landed. Jesus points out four types of soil. The seed was the same in each case. The results depended upon the soil.

The "way side" was actually a path or small road that ran through the field. Birds immediately ate those seeds, which yielded no result for the farmer. Jesus later told the disciples that this soil represented hearers who are indifferent to spiritual truth. We might describe these with the proverb "In one ear and out the other." Notice that these people do hear the Word. It simply has no effect. The stony ground represents an area with thin soil covering a hard limestone rock. Seed germinates quickly in the warm damp soil, but withers as the summer heat increases. Jesus said that these people are comfortable with spiritual matters as long as things are easy. But as soon as trouble starts, they renounce the truth and depart. The third soil is very good but has heavy dense thorns growing in it. The thorns choke the sprouting seed and again the farmer gets nothing. These hearers place more value on material possessions than on spiritual reality. Last, Jesus describes the good soil. It yields a huge harvest. Some within this group produce more than others do. These folks not only hear the Word of God, they respond to it. The farmer obviously delights in the rich harvest.

28

### Exercise: What's Your Soil Type?

**Goal:** To encourage self-examination and motivation for change as needed.

**Procedures:** Divide the class into four groups and assign each a soil type as found in the parable of the soils. Write the four types on the board in separate columns and include a very brief description of the main characteristics of each. Have groups describe the actions and attitudes of modern teens of each soil type. Write several answers for each type on the board. Ask the students to mentally put themselves in the proper group according to their actions and attitudes. Stress that a positive response to God's Word can change their categories.

What was Jesus trying to teach in the parable of the soils? He explained each major part to the disciples in Mark 4:14-20.

Notice that the farmer spread seed on every part of his field. God intends that every man hear His Word.

The result depends upon the soil. If we push the details of the story too far, we might conclude that a man is incapable of producing a harvest or a suitable response to the Word due to his surroundings. "I cannot be responsible for the rock under me," could be interpreted as "God made me with a love for things, therefore I cannot respond to His Word." Jesus told the story so that the serious hearers would recognize the dangers of casual religion, emotionalism, and materialism. They can then weed those things out of their lives and become productive for the Lord.

Notice also that Jesus tells two additional shorter stories as footnotes to the parable of the soils. Each of these reinforces the idea that change is possible. In Mark 4:21, 22 Jesus relates a common scene in the ancient world.

People lit small oil lamps at night and placed them on a candlestick to give light to the household. Jesus tells them that just as the lamp gives light to the darkness, so God wants to reveal the hidden things of His Word to all who will receive it. He does not want to conceal the good news of salvation. He simply states it so that those who are dull of hearing have a better opportunity to understand it over time. The key is to respond properly. Notice in the next story that those who hear and respond properly are given more truth (Mark 4:24, 25). Change is possible as we listen and apply the Word to our lives. The parables hid truth to those who refused it and exposed truth to those who wanted it.

29

### Parable of the Growing Seed

Jesus' next parable related truth that was both familiar and perplexing to the farmer. He simply stated in the story that God's kingdom grows like a seed planted in the ground. The plant passes through normal stages of development. It sprouts, grows the blade, then the ear, and afterwards the grain. The farmer can then harvest the grain for his benefit. As the farmer inspects his fields day by day, he cannot understand how the seed develops and produces the harvest. It simply grows under the direction of God's power in nature.

Mature Christians often look back over their lives with amazement at how God directed them through various stages of growth. The power and energy pushing them toward the harvest was not of human origin. Jesus told Nicodemus that the Holy Spirit, like the wind, germinated the seeds of salvation in man's heart (John 3). John the Baptist proclaimed that Jesus would baptize believers with the Holy Spirit (Mark 1:8). It seems that God uses His Spirit to develop the lives of believers into a bountiful harvest. Jesus' point is that the growth is impossible to understand fully, but that it does lead to positive results. Bible scholars debate whether this growth refers to the kingdom as a whole or to individual believers. Since the kingdom is made up of individuals, it seems to apply to both. We can rejoice that God works in our lives and has a definite design for us.

### Exercise: Seed Potentials

**Goal:** To develop a vision for God's power to transform and to use ordinary people.

**Procedure:** Obtain several types of seeds and attach them to white paper so that each seed may be easily viewed. Ask the students to describe what type of plant might grow from the seed. The students should write down their answers and, once everyone is finished, share their guesses. Reveal the type of seed and then describe the plant that will grow from it. Remind the students that God can develop and use each of them. The final results may look totally different from their lives now. Encourage them to seek God's will in every area of life.

## Small Seeds for a Large Nation

J. Hudson Taylor (1832-1905) dedicated his entire adult life to reaching the millions of China. Over the years, the Lord used Hudson Taylor to raise huge sums of money for the work in China, to establish twenty mission stations with over eight hundred missionaries, and to lead thousands to Christ. His legacy of answered prayer and ceaseless work still inspires missionaries today. Equally important, Taylor was the driving force behind evangelizing a massive, pagan nation for Christ.

Two seemingly small events mark the beginning of Taylor's spiritual life. As a teenager, he had drifted away from his parents' Christian faith and values. On a day off from his work in a bank, he was bored and picked up a small gospel tract from his father's library. The title, "It is Finished," gripped his heart as he understood for the first time Christ's power to save. Little did he know at the time that his mother, who was seventy miles away, was intensely praying for his salvation that very hour. The effects of a single gospel tract and a mother's prayer eventually shook the nation of China.

What could God do through you?

## Parable of the Mustard Seed

The final parable recorded by Mark is similar to the second one. Jesus often repeated His teachings so that the disciples and others might better understand. Keep in mind that the Jews of the day looked for a strong political kingdom that would drive out foreign rulers and reestablish the nation of Israel. They wanted immediate action. Mark relates the story of the mustard plant.

The tiny seeds are placed in the ground and over time the plant grows mightily. Man uses the plant for food, and the birds

The plant that Jesus refers to is probably *sinapis coccifera*. Several varieties in this plant family are common in Palestine.

Mark 4:30 records Jesus' only use of the word *we* in the parables. It suggests that He earnestly wants the listeners to understand the parable.

31

use it for shelter. God's kingdom would start out small and hardly noticeable. At maturity, the kingdom will be great and beneficial to all. Jesus' hearers marveled at the eventual size of the mustard plant compared to its humble beginnings. In time, they would likewise understand that Jesus' ministry was simply the small and obscure beginning of the kingdom. The growth would be enormous. We can be confident that the kingdom of God will continue to grow and to prosper.

## The Kingdom for Common People

Jesus began His ministry by preaching very plainly about the kingdom of God. The Jewish religious leaders rejected Jesus' message just as they had rejected John the Baptist's. But at least for a while, the great multitudes of Galilee flocked to hear the greatest teacher ever. Jesus perceived that many did not understand and so He began to use parables to further encourage understanding and belief. One day, Jesus traveled to Nazareth, His hometown, and taught in the synagogue (Mark 6:1-6). Many family members attended the service. They could not comprehend how Jesus could teach so well and heal so many. Their failure to understand His teaching and His identity as the Christ led them to foolishly reject Him to their own peril.

> And he could there do no mighty work, save that he laid his hands upon a few sick folk, and healed them. And he marvelled because of their unbelief. And he went round about the villages, teaching (Mark 6:5, 6).

Mark indicates that the people's lack of faith limited what Jesus could do for them. Their needs remained because they responded improperly to the King. It seems too that Jesus expected better from them. They knew Him from childhood. They had plainly heard the Word of God. The miracles and healings attested to the truth of His preaching. When Jesus could do no more for them, He simply departed to tell others who perhaps would respond according to God's plan.

The majority of us are like the multitudes of Jesus' day. We hear the Word of God, and yet many times we don't understand it. A decision then confronts us. When we earnestly try to understand and to believe, we make the right choice, which yields great benefit. On the other hand, we can choose to ignore the Word. The consequences can be devastating. Jared and Tessa were puzzled at first by their father's request to find out what Jesus did in the villages. Their proper response led to a great privilege – that of sharing the gospel – and their vacation went from boring to fantastic! Jesus can fantastically transform us provided that we respond to the simple teaching of His Word.

The Gospels record that on two different occasions Jesus marveled or wondered. One case involved the faith of a Gentile centurion (Matt. 8:10). The other was the lack of faith expressed by His family and hometown friends (Mark 6:6).

33

## Discussion: Choices and Consequences

**Goal:** To examine the power of choice in the students' lives.

**Procedure:** Select people in the Bible and review their lives in terms of the choices they made to follow either the Lord or their own way. Adam, Lot, Abraham, David, Solomon, and Judas make good examples. Stress the need to listen to and to obey the Lord. As time permits, use the same procedure with a literary character, with a person currently in the news, or with a friend. Always bring the discussion back to the necessity of being teachable and following the Lord.

# Review Questions

1. Jesus was both man and what?

   **God**

2. What is man's main problem?

   **Sin**

3. In what region did Jesus begin His preaching ministry?

   **Galilee**

4. Who anticipated a king to occupy David's throne?

   **Jews**

5. Who prophesied that Galilee would see a great light?

   **Isaiah**

6. What two things do parables do with the truth?

   **Reveal and conceal**

7. What represent worldly possessions in the parable of the soils?

   **Thorns**

8. What do people who respond properly to God's Word receive more of?

   **Truth**

9. Jesus compared the kingdom to what kind of seed?

   **Mustard**

10. What was Jesus' boyhood hometown?

   *Nazareth*

11. Why was Jesus a good teacher?

   *Jesus was a good teacher because He was God and man and could relate God's truth in human terms. He also used simple, everyday stories to communicate with the common people.*

12. Why did John the Baptist and Jesus preach the common theme of repentance?

   *Man's greatest need is to turn from sin. God desires man's good, and therefore God's representatives dealt with the most basic problem in life.*

35

13. Why did the Jews dislike the Romans?

   *The Romans controlled the government and the Jews believed it belonged to them. The Romans also provoked the Jews with many pagan practices.*

14. How do people enter God's kingdom?

   *People must repent of their sins and believe the gospel to enter the kingdom of God.*

15. What is casual religion?

   *Casual religion is practiced by people who hear the word of God and do not allow it to affect their lives.*

# CHAPTER THREE

# Christ and the Sick

John Sizemore and his group of friends piled onto the bus with about twenty other juniors and seniors. The bus headed toward the Nelson home, which was about five miles into the country from the church. Everyone looked forward to the monthly Sunday evening singspirations and especially to the food. Several cars were already in the driveway as the bus pulled up. Some of the guys immediately started the usual basketball game while the girls gathered around the patio to talk. In about thirty minutes the pizza arrived and Mr. Nelson called the teens into the house. Once inside, John noticed three or four people that he did not know. After prayer, the guys waited impatiently for the girls to get their pizza, chips, and drink. The Nelsons then quickly moved out of the way as fourteen hungry young men reduced five large pepperoni pizzas to empty cardboard boxes.

"Do you guys always eat like this?" asked one of the girls that John did not know.

After wiping the pizza sauce off his fingers, John extended his hand and formally introduced himself to Megan Matthews. She was visiting her uncle for a couple of weeks and really seemed to enjoy the large group of teens.

After the food, the youth pastor led the teens in several hymns and choruses. He then asked if anyone had a prayer request or a testimony that he wanted to share. Megan shyly raised her hand and began to speak, "This has been a great evening for me! My church in Grand Junction is very small. We have maybe five teens, so we don't often do much together. Praise the Lord that we

## Goals

Students should

1. Prepare to face illness.
2. Recognize Christ's power over illness.
3. Understand God's use of illness.

## Objectives

Students should be able to

1. Analyze historical Scripture passages for meaning.
2. Identify examples of Christ's compassion.
3. Explain the priority of spiritual needs over physical illness.
4. State the role of faith in illness.
5. Discuss how illness can draw men to God.

## Scripture Reading

1. Mark 1–8
2. Isaiah 53
3. Leviticus 13, 14

## Memory Verses

1. Mark 1:41
2. Mark 5:36
3. Ephesians 3:20

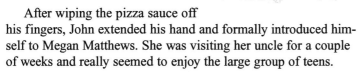

## Lecture Overview

### Introduction

1. All will face illness.
2. Christ gives us the path to victory.

### Lessons at Peter's House

1. Peter's mother-in-law
2. Multitudes
3. Christ's priority

### Lessons with a Leper

1. Misery of leprosy
2. Power of Christ
3. Compassion of Christ

### Lessons with a Leader

1. Faith tested
2. Power revealed

### Lessons with a Lady

1. Faith purified
2. Power revealed

### Our Situation Today

1. Review Christ's person, power, and compassion.
2. Relationship with God

Note that many discussion ideas and other exercises are provided for use at the teacher's discretion.

**Day 1** Class reading of Mark

Homework: Read Student Text Chapter 3

**Day 2** Introductory exercises, Lessons at Peter's House and Lessons with a Leper lecture

**Day 3** Leprosy in the Bible worksheet

**Day 4** Lessons with a Leader and Lessons with a Lady lecture

**Day 5** You Are the Teacher worksheet

**Thoughts for the Teacher**

1. The emphasis on reading the text of Mark will provide valuable general knowledge of the Scripture.

2. Some of the students will have personal experience with serious illness. Others will not. Being sensitive to both groups will open many ministry opportunities.

3. Draw sharp distinctions between Christ's ministry and modern faith healers.

4. Continually focus the class on the person and work of Christ. Contrast Christ's power with religion, illness, and fear.

5. Space does not permit the treatment of every healing in Mark. The appendix contains an exercise on some of the omitted material. Also, see the list of passages on healings later in this chapter.

can sing and have a great time together. You might remember to pray for my mom. She has a disease that is very painful. I can hardly pronounce its name. God has been very good to us in every way."

John "worked things out" so that he sat near Megan on the bus ride back to the church. He asked her how she could be so calm and peaceful while talking about her mother.

Megan responded, "It's not always easy for sure. The Lord is teaching us that this illness is simply a tool to teach us more about trusting Him. I often don't understand things, but every morning my dad reminds us that God is good and I believe it."

Sickness and disease tend to be very impersonal and far off until a friend or relative is in serious physical trouble. Cancer may become a daily issue. The care of an accident victim may change our plans for school. Heart disease may restrict activity and travel. The death of a family member may change everything. Illness and death are a very real part of life.

Megan and her family fought daily battles with her mother's illness. One day, unless the Lord dramatically intervenes, you will face a similar battle. Mark records many times when Jesus encountered either the ill or their friends and family. Jesus was able to view their conflict from God's perspective and also from man's. His actions and teachings help us to understand illness for what it is and then how to deal with it. His view may surprise you. As we believe and put His thoughts into practice, the Lord will prepare us for genuine victory when dealing with physical maladies. The length of this book will not permit an in-depth study of each situation. We can, however, examine a few key passages and start learning how Jesus responded to human illness.

38

Note: Any one of the next three exercises may be used to introduce the class to the subject of physical illness.

### Exercise: Disease in the Headlines!

**Goal:** To introduce the reality of physical illness.

**Procedure:** Obtain newspapers or magazines for several different days. Instruct the students to find stories about or references to medical issues and share the results with the class. Emphasize the prevalence of illness.

### Exercise: Personal Testimony

**Goal:** To introduce the reality of physical illness.

**Procedure:** Choose one or two students that you know have experienced medical problems either personally or in their families. In private, ask them to tell you about the situation. As appropriate, allow them three to five minutes to talk to the class about their experience. Emphasize the prevalence of illness.

### Exercise: Medical Work

**Goal:** To introduce the reality of physical illness.

**Procedure:** Ask a medical professional to talk to the class about the nature of sickness and disease. Prior to the class, instruct the speaker about your goals and desires for the presentation. Allow

## Lessons at Peter's House
### Mark 1:29-39

Mark continually shows us that Jesus kept a very busy schedule. Jesus started the day by teaching with great authority in the synagogue at Capernaum. He then cast out an unclean spirit from a man in the assembly. The news of these mighty deeds soon spread through all Galilee. Peter evidently invited Him to his home for the customary Sabbath meal, which was much like our Sunday dinner. The disciples told Jesus about Peter's mother-in-law and her fever. He entered her room, took her by the hand, and raised her up. The fever departed and she began to minister to them. Perhaps she prepared the meal. She took no medicines. There was not a period of convalescence. In the privacy of Peter's home, Jesus completely healed this woman.

Mark does not record the specific reactions of the people in the house. We can assume that they were utterly astonished. Not

See Luke 4:38-44 for a parallel account. Notice that Luke describes the illness as a "great fever," or burning.

Alfred Edersheim's *The Life and Times of Jesus the Messiah* (Eerdmans, Grand Rapids, Michigan, 1977) provides good insight into NT practices at the time of Christ. The reading may be tedious at times, but the information is outstanding. See Book III, page 486 for a discussion of Jewish remedies for fevers.

39

the students to ask questions. Emphasize the need to consider medical issues before they develop.

### Exercise: Medical Remedies

**Goal:** To contrast the power of Christ with modern medical remedies.

**Procedure:** Instruct the students to look up medical remedies for various problems. This research may be assigned as homework or class work. The Internet, medical encyclopedias, and textbooks will provide good material. Allow several students to share their findings with the class. Direct the students' attention to the simplicity of Mark's statements about Christ's healings. Emphasize the deity and power of Christ.

### Exercise: Repent!

**Goal:** To review the biblical teaching on repentance.

**Procedure:** Divide the class into groups of three to five students. Assign each group one set of passages from the list below. Have the groups decide the general theme of their passages. In each case the theme is repentance. Instruct the students to create a two- to three-minute role-playing presentation about ordinary life that represents repentance or a change of direction. An example might be making a wrong turn on a road and needing to turn around to go in the right direction. Allow the students to make only could Jesus teach with great power, but His simple touch could heal sickness. The Jewish traditions of the day prescribed a remedy for this ailment. A person would tie an iron knife to a thorn bush using a lock of hair. He would then repeat certain Old Testament verses and cut down the bush. Christ's power, compassion, and simplicity stood in stark contrast to the mystical treatments of the rabbis.

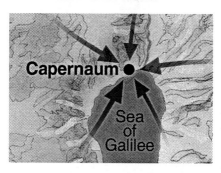

Mark 1:32 *Brought* is an imperfect verb meaning "continually brought." The healing session evidently was very long.

Jesus immediately became the focus of attention in Peter's house and in all Capernaum. The people heard Him teach in the morning and heard that He healed a fever in the afternoon. At the end of the Sabbath day when people could travel, they started bringing the sick and diseased to Peter's door. Jesus healed each one. The variety of medical problems did not impede His work. Mark does not tell us how Jesus did it. His compassionate care may have extended well into the night.

The next paragraph reveals more of Jesus' purposes (Mark 1:35-39). The phrase "a great while before morning" refers to the fourth watch of the night or between 3 and 6 A.M. Jesus hid Himself outside the city in order to pray. Peter finally found Him and reported that the multitudes also looked for Him. Most teachers or healers would rejoice in such an enthusiastic following, but Jesus did not. It seems that for the time His work was completed in Capernaum. His desire and passion was to preach the gospel of the kingdom: man must repent of sins and believe. The miraculous healings gave credibility to the message of Christ. The physical need became the path to the spiritual opportunity. As God, Jesus knew that man's sin problem had eternal consequences. Man's physical problems are of this world. Although healing the body helped for a short while, preaching the gospel could save man forever. "And he preached in their synagogues throughout all Galilee, and cast out devils" (Mark 1:39). This verse directs our attention to Christ's routine of preaching and dealing with other needs.

The Romans divided the twelve hours of night into four distinct watches. A soldier would be responsible to stand guard over the city or soldiers in the field for a single watch. It appears that the Jews followed the Roman format. See Mark 6:48.

Scholars debate the length of time Jesus spent on the tour of Galilee. "Throughout all Galilee" indicates a long period of ministry. Perhaps one of Jesus' purposes was to continually show His power and compassion to the disciples. Eventually, Jesus would send them out on their own.

the presentation to the class and ask the class to choose the best one. At the end, emphasize that repentance is a change of direction and a change of mind about sin.

Passages:

1. Deuteronomy 4:29-31; Luke 10:13; Romans 2:4

2. II Chronicles 7:14; Matthew 10:13; James 4:8-10

3. Nehemiah 1:8, 9; Acts 2:38-40; II Corinthians 7:9-11

4. Job 42:1-6; Acts 20:21; Hebrews 6:1

## World Religions and Medicine

HISTORICAL LIGHT

The connection between medical practice and religion has persisted from ancient civilizations to modern times. Encyclopedias and medical books contain many fascinating and sometimes grotesque accounts of medical procedures.

Mesopotamia: Priests examined animal and human intestines to manipulate spirits that caused illness. Hammurabi's law code specified severe punishments for doctors who failed to heal their patients. A surgeon whose patient died could have his hand cut off.

India: The Vedas, sacred Hindu writings, prescribed magical practices and incantations to remove demons that caused disease and other disorders. Surgeons used alcoholic drinks to ease pain and tar to seal incisions.

China: Chinese medical practices centered on the balance and control of yin and yang in the body. Like other things, the body consisted of wood, fire, earth, metal, and water. Careful interpretation of the pulse could determine the state of health and could predict the date of death. Herbal remedies and acupuncture helped maintain physical balances.

Greece: Asclepius, god of medicine, reportedly could heal those who came to his temples for baths and sleep. As the patients slept and dreamed, Asclepius gave them some particular cure. Hippocrates, the father of modern medicine, used honey as a primary medical treatment. He also drilled holes into people's heads to relieve pressure and sickness.

The Internet and various encyclopedias contain much good information on the history of medicine. Students could research one or more areas in preparation for a class discussion.

Note that Mark does not give reasons for any particular illness. The emphasis is on the power and compassion of Christ. Scripture ultimately attributes illness to sin in Genesis 3. God also uses physical illness to glorify Himself and teach us. See John 11:4 and Job 42:1-6.

The particular cases of physical affliction associated with demon possession will be addressed in the next chapter.

41

Leprosy in the Bible can refer to a variety of afflictions. Modern medicine identifies leprosy as the disease caused by the bacillus *mycobacterium leprae*. Doctors disagree on how well current antibiotic treatment works. As was the case in the ancient world, leprosy continues to be a dreaded disease. Descriptions of people with advanced leprosy can be very repulsive. Use additional information found on the Internet about the physical reality of the disease to underscore the power of Christ in cleansing the leper.

See Edersheim, Book III, page 495 for a discussion of leprosy in the ancient world.

## *L*essons with a Leper
### Mark 1:40-45

Leprosy—or Hansen's disease, as it is known today—is an affliction that most of us have not seen. Modern medical researchers believe that infected people spread the disease through discharges from the nose and mouth. Numbness, skin discoloration, and severe disfiguration may not appear for years after the initial infection. Doctors discovered the first effective drug treatment for leprosy in the 1940s. Most cases today occur in very poor areas of the world.

People in the ancient world dreaded leprosy and took significant action to restrain its spread. The Old Testament contains information on diagnosing and controlling it. Lepers were ceremonially unclean and were to be isolated from the rest of the Israelites according to Leviticus 13 and 14. Rabbis called leprosy "walking death" and had no cures for it. One rabbi said that he kept a separation of at least six feet from any leper and one hundred feet if the leper was upwind. He also threw rocks at them to keep them away. Most people associated leprosy with sin and the effects of sin.

Bible scholars do not know how many lepers lived in Palestine during Jesus' ministry. Based on general references in the New Testament and in other literature at the time, Jesus presumably saw lepers fairly often. They probably avoided Him as they would avoid the rabbis and other people.

42

---

### Worksheet:
### Leprosy in the Bible

**Goal:** To consider the serious nature of sin and the greatness of God's power.

**Procedure:** Duplicate the Leprosy in the Bible worksheet in the Appendix (pp. 144-45). After the students complete the worksheet, start a discussion about what triggered God's judgment. Next, discuss God's methods and power in healing. Emphasize that leprosy is a picture of sin, and that God can cleanse the most polluted sinner.

### Discussion:
### What is Compassion?

**Goal:** To develop compassion for others.

**Procedure:** Read one or more dictionary definitions of compassion. Ask the students to describe Christ's compassion for the sick. Next, ask them to describe how a typical teenager views the sick. Note the differences. Emphasize that true compassion meets the needs of others. Challenge the students to act in the best interests of others and to deny themselves. Remind them that compassion toward people who have physical needs could yield many opportunities to meet spiritual needs.

Mark's account of Jesus' meeting with the leper is remarkable. It shows us Jesus' compassion for the sick. This man's focus on Christ reveals his faith. He had evidently seen or heard about Jesus' power to heal people. The leper approached Christ, knelt down, and humbly asked to be cleansed. He acknowledged Christ's power and desired His mercy. Christ touched him and said, "I will; be thou clean." The religious leaders and common people would never touch a leper for fear of contamination. Touching a leper would also make the individual ceremonially unclean. As the Son of God, Jesus' touch removed the defilement and immediately created a bond of compassion and comfort with the man. The healing was immediate.

The next verses show Jesus' intense compassion for this leper. Remember that the healings drew great crowds. Many wanted physical relief more than they wanted spiritual instruction. As God, Jesus knew man's inward motives, and He knew what this cleansed leper would do. The Greek verb translated "straitly charged" comes from a root that means "snort like a horse." Horses snort when they want to get someone's attention and when they want to communicate something very serious. Jesus told the healed man to do two things. First, he was not to tell anyone about the cleansing. From that we can assume that they were alone. Jesus worked quietly in this situation. He did not want the crowds thronging him for healing. Second, the man was to follow Moses' law for the ceremonial declaration of cleansing from leprosy. He should show himself to "the priest." The definite article with *priest* indicates that this was the high priest in Jerusalem. The high priest would certainly ask about the remarkable healing and the man could offer a specific testimony of Christ's power. By this time in Jesus' ministry, the religious leadership in Jerusalem opposed Him. The testimony of the cleansed leper would remind these people that Jesus was no ordinary teacher. It would also show them that Jesus wanted to confirm the law. The man departed and told everyone what Jesus had done for him. Jesus could no longer enter the city and preach the gospel due to the notoriety. As a man, Jesus' empathy and compassion for the hopeless leper led to the cleansing. Jesus would not turn away this man with such a great need and with equally great faith.

Christ often touched people who were ceremonially unclean. Many believed that the very presence of deity removed uncleanness. People often wanted to touch Christ or they wanted Christ to touch them.

See Mark 1:41; 3:10; 5:27, 28, 30, 31; 6:56; 7:33; 8:22; 10:13.

Also, see the account of Isaiah's cleansing in Isaiah 6.

Verses that indicate Jesus' knowledge about the people and circumstances around Him include the following: John 2:24, 25; 6:64; 16:30. Each case points to Christ's deity.

Jesus' purpose was not to destroy the law but to fulfill it. See Matthew 5:17. His instruction to the leper ties back to Leviticus 14.

43

The context of Mark 5:21 indicates that Jesus was very busy. It seems that the accusation of the leaders in Mark 3:21-29, the family inquiry in Mark 3:31-35, the teaching and miracle at sea in Mark 4, and the events in Gadara in Mark 5 all occurred in just a few days. Again, Mark shows us glimpses of Christ's busy ministry. We can assume that the times not recorded were also busy.

Many students fail to see the need for English and literature courses. Viewing the Gospels as literature will help the students to comprehend the meaning. Of course, the liberal view that the Bible is only a literary work like that of Plato or Shakespeare is to be rejected.

The local synagogue ruler determined the order of service and the participants for religious events. Some large synagogues had more than one ruler.

The verb tenses in Mark 5:24 paint a dramatic picture of the scene. *Went* is an aorist and indicates a one-time action. The idea is that Jesus immediately left the shore to go with Jairus. *Followed* and *thronged* are imperfect verbs indicating incomplete or continual actions. The crowd probably hindered Jesus' every step. This may have allowed the woman to catch up and to touch Him.

See the following verses on the importance of faith for a relationship with God: Genesis 15:6; Exodus 4:5; Isaiah 7:9; Habakkuk 2:4.

## Lessons with a Leader
### Mark 5:21-24, 35-43

The account of Jairus's daughter provides additional insight into Jesus' attitude about sickness and death. Your literature instructor may teach you to analyze a story for the meaning or for the author's purpose in writing it. When analyzing this story, we see that Jesus is certainly the main character. Some may assert

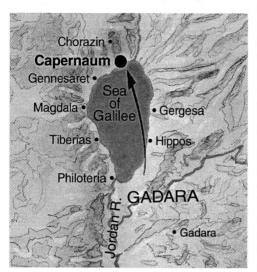

that the second primary character is the little girl. Notice, however, that the girl is entirely passive relative to the details provided by Mark. She was sick and later died. The most dynamic details concern Jairus himself. Jesus' words to him, "Be not afraid, only believe," seem to be the point of the narrative. Faith is not an end in itself. Faith builds a relationship between God and man. The infirmity of the daughter is the means or the tool that Jesus uses to strengthen Jairus's faith.

Let's examine some of the details. Jesus had just returned from a trip to Gadara on the other side of the Sea of Galilee. Huge crowds met him on the shore, which indicates that His popularity with the common people continued to grow. Jairus, a ruler of the synagogue, met Him with a most urgent request. In Mark 3:22, Jewish leaders had traveled to Galilee from Jerusalem and accused Jesus of working for Satan. Jairus, due to his rank, may have been aware of this accusation. But he also knew about Jesus' power to heal. The desperate condition of his daughter compelled him to break through the crowds and ask Jesus to heal her. Notice Jairus's emotion as recorded by his words "little daughter" and "point of death." The Greek grammar indicates that Jesus immediately departed with him and that the multitudes continually hindered

44

## Exercise: Literary Insight

**Goal:** To use standard literary techniques to interpret Scripture.

**Procedures:** Ask the students to learn basic principles of literary analysis. Instruct the students to analyze a passage from Mark using the principles.

For example, they should discover the setting (place, time, culture), the protagonist (one who initiates action) and antagonist (one who reacts to action), and the climax of action or interest.

An English teacher may be able to help, if needed. The students' goal is to decide what main point the author intended in a particular narrative. The students will gain much from careful thought about the Scriptures.

their progress. Jairus's joy concerning Jesus' decision was quickly dashed by the delay with the woman. We will examine her case later. News came that the daughter had died. We can assume from human experience that Jairus lost all hope. Jesus encouraged him to believe and continued the journey. Professional mourners with their howls and shrieks of grief met them at the house.

Jesus communicated His intention to help the girl and they scornfully laughed at Him. Jairus's actions show that he believed Jesus. The mourners did not believe and were thus expelled from the house. Jesus touched the little girl as He had touched the leper. He then uttered "Talitha cumi," a common phrase in the everyday Aramaic language that means "Daughter, arise." These may have been the same words used by Jewish mothers when

*Typical synagogue*

45

Professional mourners were always at funerals in ancient Palestine. Even the poor hired at least one or two wailing women and a flute player. Jairus was a ruler and perhaps a man of some wealth, therefore there were probably many mourners. Since the funeral was already in progress when Jesus arrived, we may assume that Jairus had expected the child to die and thus he had made the arrangements.

This is the first time that Jesus singled out Peter, James, and John to witness an event. Deuteronomy 17:6 required two or three witnesses to attest to the truthfulness of a claim. Jesus may have chosen them to tell others about this semi-private event.

### Discussion: Key Words

**Goal:** To remember important statements in the Scripture.

**Procedures:** Ask the students to share with the class the most memorable words of their parents, coach, friend, neighbor, etc. Having the students write the responses so that the teacher can select and read them might keep the class under better control. Point out that Jesus' words *Talitha cumi* made a great impression upon those who saw the miracle. Share with the class the words of Scripture that challenge you the most. "It is finished" gripped Hudson Taylor. "The just shall live by his faith" was Martin Luther's motivation.

### Ministering to the Sick

Following Christ's example means, in part, ministering to the sick. You have a great opportunity to help people in your own age group. Fear is the main reason that Christians fail in this area. As a teen, always seek the advice of a parent or spiritual leader before proceeding. Ask about the person's needs and then formulate a plan to help. Something as simple as a friendly chat or gathering homework assignments can be great encouragement. Every situation is different, so flexibility is vital. Always try to communicate God's Word and show compassion.

waking their children from sleep in the morning. Mark's inclusion of the specific phrase points to the deep impression that the words made on the hearers. Christ's touch and words raised a girl from the dead. The people in the house were astonished. We get the English word "ecstasy" from Mark's description of their reaction. Their joy and delight over the daughter's new life led to a deeper relationship with the Christ, the source of all life. Jesus told them not to spread the details around the community so that He could continue His preaching ministry. He also asked them to give the girl something to eat. Even in the smallest details, Jesus showed His compassion for those in need.

### *L*essons with a Lady
#### Mark 5:24-34

We might say that Jairus's faith was initially weak and many enemies attacked it. In the end, his faith in Christ prevailed, and his daughter's life was restored. Mark records another incident, which Jairus saw. Again, the chief issue seems to be faith, or trust. Superstition and fear melted when Jesus said, "Daughter, thy faith hath made thee whole; go in peace, and be whole of thy plague" (Mark 5:34).

The description of this healing is another opportunity to emphasize grammar as the basis of understanding the Bible.

The personal nature of this lady's problem should be handled with dignity and discernment. The teacher's example and attitude while discussing it will diminish immature reactions by the students. See Leviticus 15:25-27 for a discussion of this particular uncleanness.

## Discussion: Desperate Measures

**Goal:** To encourage action to meet personal spiritual needs.

**Procedures:** Ask the students to tell the class about the actions of people or teams in desperate times. Sports teams, grades, and car problems may be used effectively. "What does a football team do when behind by four points with only three seconds to play?" The response may be to throw a long pass or to run a trick play. Most students will enjoy participating in the discussion. Turn the conversation toward the desperate situation of the woman in Mark 5:25. Point out that when sinners realize their desperate condition, they will take action to come to Christ. Emphasize the need for a faith that acts decisively.

Hospital visits can be especially scary. Here are some suggestions to help:

1. Do not visit alone. Enlist the help of a friend or family member.

2. Stop at the visitors' information desk and ask about specific regulations and guidelines for your visit. Obeying the rules will help you to gain the respect of the medical professionals and will make the visit easier.

3. Keep the visit fairly short. Ask the patient to tell you when he or she is tired or when you should leave the room for other reasons.

4. End the visit if the patient is in severe pain, is being actively treated, or is eating. Assure him that you will come back at a more appropriate time.

5. Don't try to help with medical procedures. Summon the hospital staff for the need.

6. Remember that you are God's servant and that your purpose is to show compassion and concern. Be cheerful and positive.

7. Ask if you can pray with your friend before departing. Be brief and specific.

8. Ask if you can take care of some need outside the hospital. Follow through on anything reasonable that is asked.

9. Set up another time when you can visit the patient either in the hospital or at home.

10. Always wash your hands after exiting the hospital building.

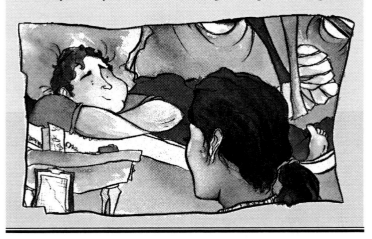

The longest sentence in Mark's Gospel describes the condition of the lady with an issue of blood. A good way to understand a complicated sentence is to find the simple subject, the verb, and then the object. The other parts will be understood as modifying one of the essential parts. In Mark 5:25-27, the basic sentence with a few modifiers included for clarity is, "A woman touched his garment."

The intervening words communicate her history. Her name and specific identity are not given. She may have been a stranger to the folks in the town. According to Leviticus 15:25-27, those in her condition were ceremonially unclean, along with anyone who touched them. It seems reasonable that after so many years of illness, people would know of her situation and would demand her separation from the crowds. The woman tried everything possible to heal the affliction. The Talmud, a collection of Jewish traditions, records eleven different remedies to stop an issue of blood. Perhaps the local doctors used one or more of these treatments. Nothing worked and she became worse. Upon hearing about Jesus, the woman traveled to the town and worked her way through the crowds in order to touch His garment. "If I may touch but his clothes, I shall be whole"—this is the verbal expression of a faith that takes action. After coming to Him from behind, she touched Christ's outer robe. Immediately the bleeding ceased.

At this point in the narrative, most of us would conclude that the woman's problem was solved and that Jesus could now help Jairus. Jesus looked at the situation much differently. He wanted to perfect her faith and rid it of harmful elements. Jesus stopped and asked, "Who touched my clothes?" The disciples thought that His question was ridiculous since the crowd pressed upon Him. Jesus continued to look for the woman until she came and

The Talmud is a collection of Jewish oral teachings and traditions about Jewish life and events in the Old Testament. Most parts were assembled from the second to the sixth centuries A.D. Though some parts of the Talmud do not directly relate to the situation in Jesus' time, the writings do give a good picture of Jewish thinking on many issues.

Christ's words to the woman, "thy faith hath made thee whole," negate the value of objects associated with Christ. The Roman Catholic Church and others believe that pieces of wood, bone, and cloth have spiritual power and significance. Jesus kindly rebuked the superstitious faith of the woman. Believers must reject any practice that draws attention away from Christ Himself and exalts an object.

See Edersheim, Book III, page 620 for ancient remedies for an issue of blood.

confessed her actions. The text implies that she told Him the whole story of her affliction. Jesus addresses her as "daughter" which implies a close relationship. He reinforces the concept of a relationship by telling her that her faith, not the superstitious touching of a piece of cloth, healed her. Many ancient remedies used rituals and enchantments. His search for her led to the personal relationship that was much more important than the physical healing. The phrase "go in peace" might better be translated "go into peace," which indicates a much brighter future for the woman than she could imagine before her meeting with Jesus. The text also indicates that while Jesus spoke to her, the message arrived about Jairus's daughter. The attention of the crowd turned away from her, thus protecting her privacy. She could enjoy her newfound health without questions from the crowd. Once again, Jesus showed compassion even in the smallest details.

49

## PRINCIPLES APPLIED

## Fanny Crosby: Blind Yet Believing

Fanny Crosby (1820-1915) lost her sight as an infant when a phony doctor prescribed the wrong ointment for an eye problem. She later attended and taught at the New York Institute for the Blind. A cholera epidemic struck the city and the school in 1849. Many students died. The tragedies made Fanny realize that she knew about God, but did not know God personally. She trusted Christ at a revival meeting. A few years later, sorrow once again visited when her only child died in infancy.

Sickness and sorrow often make people bitter and resentful against God. Fanny Crosby's poetry reveals her unfailing faith in God's goodness and sovereignty. Great human affliction and sorrow became God's tool to fill Christian hymnals with songs of praise. Notice that Fanny Crosby emphasizes the Lord's character and grace in her popular "All the Way My Savior Leads Me."

All the way my Savior leads me;
What have I to ask beside?
Can I doubt His tender mercy,
Who through life has been my Guide?
Heavenly peace, divinest comfort,
Here by faith in Him to dwell!
For I know, whate'er befall me,
Jesus doeth all things well.

All the way my Savior leads me,
Cheers each winding path I tread,
Gives me grace for every trial,
Feeds me with the living bread.
Though my weary steps may falter
And my soul athirst may be,
Gushing from the Rock before me,
Lo! A spring of joy I see.

All the way my Savior leads me;
Oh, the fullness of His love!
Perfect rest to me is promised
In my Father's house above.
When my spirit, clothed immortal,
Wings its flight to realms of day,
This my song through endless ages:
Jesus led me all the way.

## *O*ur Situation Today

Let's review what we have learned about Jesus' ministry to the sick. At Peter's home, Jesus proved that He had the power to heal all types of illness. His actions, however, showed that His priority was not the healing of the body but the saving of the soul through preaching. The miracles of healing gave visual and powerful credibility to His messages in the synagogues. The incident with the leper in Galilee showed Christ's enormous compassion for the physical needs of man. His care and power contrasted with the hatefulness of the religious leaders of that time. In Jairus's case, we see Jesus not only dealing with the death of a child but also strengthening the weak faith of a very religious man. The woman with the issue of blood had faith, but it was marred by superstition.

Christ healed her body and purified her faith. Mark records nine specific people that Jesus healed. He also shows us in four passages that Jesus' normal routine included curing sickness of every sort. Relieving human suffering played an important part in Christ's ministry.

God in His wisdom provided us with details of Christ's life so that we might understand His thinking about our lives. Learning Christ's lessons on illness will bring great peace and quietness during difficult times, which are certain to come. Let's first remember the theological purpose of Christ's healing ministry. His actions contrasted with the dead religion of the day and pointed to

Specific people that Jesus healed in Mark include:

Peter's mother-in-law (1:29-31)

Leper (1:40-45)

Palsied man (2:1-12)

Man with a withered hand (3:1-5)

Jairus's daughter (5:21-24, 35-43)

Woman with the issue of blood (5:25-34)

Deaf man (7:31-37)

Blind man (8:22-26)

Blind Bartimaeus (10:46-52)

Passages indicating Jesus healed many people include:

Galilee (1:32-34)

Galilee (3:10)

Nazareth (6:5, 6)

Gennesaret (6:53-56)

51

---

### Worksheet: Reporters in Action

**Goal:** To analyze other healings in Mark.

**Procedure:** See the Reporters in Action worksheet in the Appendix (p. 146). Assign each student a passage in Mark that records one of Christ's healing miracles. The worksheet uses simple journalistic questions to expose the details and meanings of the verses. Not every question will require a lengthy answer.

Consult a commentary such as *Mark, A Portrait of the Servant* by Hiebert for help with difficult areas. A grade based on effort will encourage significant student participation. This worksheet could also be assigned as homework.

Passages: Mark 2:1-12; 3:1-7; 7:31-37; 8:22-26; 10:46-52.

### Exercise: Show Compassion!

**Goal:** To provide a structured opportunity to show compassion to the sick.

**Exercise:** Set up a field trip or an after-school activity to a nursing home, hospital, children's home, or other suitable location. Set a goal that each student talk to at least three people and then find a way to help at least one. Encourage the students to share their testimonies and to witness for Christ. As a follow-up, start a class

The lack of detail in the Bible about medical issues and procedures does not give credence to those who reject medical intervention based on religious grounds. One conclusion from the verses is that the authors presume medical care for those in need.

Many pastors and Christian leaders will testify to miraculous healings today. Genuine examples seem to be in private and connected to Christian service. A detailed explanation of modern healings is not within the scope of this book and would be a distraction from the central issue of Christ.

## Answers

**Proverbs 17:22**  Merry heart

**Isaiah 1:6**  Ointment

**Isaiah 38:21**  Lump of figs

**Jeremiah 8:22**  Balm

**Ezekiel 47:12**  Leaf

**Luke 10:34**  Oil and wine

**I Timothy 5:23**  Wine

### HISTORICAL LIGHT

### Medicines in the Bible

The Bible is a book of theology. Medical issues support God's communication to us but are not a main focus of the Scriptures. The Lord can certainly heal our sicknesses, but He expects us to use appropriate means for physical health. Most of us are very thankful for adequate health-care and modern medicines. Look up the following verses and state the treatment being used.

Proverbs 17:22 _____

Isaiah 1:6 _____

Isaiah 38:21 _____

Jeremiah 8:22 _____

Ezekiel 47:12 _____

Luke 10:34 _____

I Timothy 5:23 _____

the fact that He was the Messiah. Only God had such great power over the worst diseases and even over death. "Surely he hath borne our griefs, and carried our sorrows" (Isaiah 53:4) may refer to Christ's healing ministry. Just as Christ could heal physical sickness, so we may be confident that He can dismiss the power of sin. His actions give credibility to both His person and His words.

Other purposes of Christ's healing seem to center on a fuller relationship with God. The miracles were never an end in themselves. Sinners saw Christ's great power and many were more eager to hear Him as a result. Many people will not consider spiritual truth until their body fails. Believers often realize their utter dependence upon God when cancer or disease develops. Our physical problems must point us toward greater dependence upon God. Illness does not communicate God's displeasure but rather His everlasting love. The unsaved see life as an end in itself, but Christians look forward to eternal fellowship with God in heaven. If sickness and disease can draw me closer to God, then I can face

discussion on the students' impressions and activities. Compare their efforts to Christ's.

the malady with a bright hope of better times possibly on earth and certainly in heaven.

As representatives of Christ, we can and should follow His example in dealing with the sick. Christians cannot heal people the way Christ did. We can, however, show compassion by specific acts of kindness and concern. If the purpose of sickness is to cultivate a better relationship to God, then presenting God's Word to those in need must be a priority. Believers can also assure those in need that God does indeed love them. Focusing on the eternal results of physical illness gives us the tool to handle the troublesome days that illness may bring.

# Review Questions

A. Greece        F. Hansen's disease
B. Fever         G. Jewish writings
C. Jesus         H. Howl
D. Vedas        I. Ruler
E. Fanny Crosby   J. Meeting place

**B** 1. Mother-in-law

**A** 2. Asclepius

**I** 3. Jairus

**G** 4. Talmud

**C** 5. Messiah

**D** 6. India

**F** 7. Leprosy

**H** 8. Mourner

**E** 9. Blind

**J** 10. Synagogue

11. Why did Jesus leave Capernaum in Mark 1?

*Jesus left Capernaum to preach in other places. Many people in the city still had physical needs. Jesus' priority was to preach in each place.*

12. How did Jesus' approach to healing differ from that of pagan religions?

*Jesus used healing to show compassion and to minister to spiritual needs. His touch and words were the agents of healing. In pagan religions, healers tried to manipulate spirits or balance bodily functions for physical relief.*

13. Why would a leper be considered "unclean"?

*Lepers were unclean because of the potential to spread the infection. The disease also symbolized sin and the associated pollution. God specified to Moses the procedures for dealing with the uncleanness associated with leprosy.*

14. What obstacles did Jairus's faith overcome in Mark 5?

*Jairus overcame the possible slander of Christ by the Jewish leaders. He also spoke to Jesus only after moving through a great crowd. He could have easily quit. Also, the woman with the issue of blood slowed progress. His daughter's death and the mocking of the mourners might have hindered his faith.*

15. In what way was the woman with the issue of blood exercising a superstitious faith?

*She believed that simply touching Jesus' garment would heal her. Jesus taught her that the healing came as a result of her faith.*

# CHAPTER FOUR

# Christ and the Forces of Evil
4

Reuben Mason rested on one knee as sweat dripped down his face and soaked his gym shirt. The university gym seemed unusually hot that day. The physical education teacher blew the whistle signaling the end of that wrestling match and the beginning of the next. Reuben knew that his turn to wrestle the largest and strongest guy in the class would come in just a few minutes. His mind wandered back to about three years earlier when he had had to take wrestling in high school. The very same thing had happened. On the last day of class, the teacher organized a tournament. He drew names from a bag to determine the first-round opponents. Reuben's adversary was huge. The match lasted exactly twenty-eight seconds. He could not remember whether he had been happier that the match was over or that he endured for so long. It could have been over much sooner.

The shrill whistle jarred Reuben's mind back to the task at hand. As the guys approached the center of the mat, the coach reminded them of the rules. Just before the action started, one of Reuben's friends yelled out, "I'm glad it's you and not me!"

Reuben quickly retorted, "Look at the tournament board. You get the winner of this round!"

This time, the match lasted fifteen seconds. Reuben's opponent went on to crush everyone else in the class. No one stood much of a chance against this big, strong guy who enjoyed

## Goals

Students should

1. Discern the power of Christ.
2. Be encouraged that victory is possible.
3. Establish a vital relationship with Christ.
4. Develop solid Bible study skills.

## Objectives

Students should be able to

1. Recognize characteristics of evil.
2. Identify the means of Christ's power.
3. Explain the role of faith in spiritual victory.
4. Evaluate their faith in Christ's power.

## Scripture Reading

1. Mark 9-16
2. Ephesians 6
3. I Samuel 17

## Memory Verses

1. Mark 5:19
2. Mark 9:24
3. Ephesians 6:13

## Lesson Plans

**Day 1** Class reading of Mark

Homework: Read Student Text Chapter 4

**Day 2** Introduction, Basics of the Battle lecture

**Day 3** Christ's Transforming Power worksheet

**Day 4** Chapter lecture

**Day 5** Faith Builders, Teen Struggles discussions

## Lecture Overview

### Introduction

1. The struggle against sin
2. Christ's victory over sin

### Basics of the Battle

1. Satan, the enemy
2. Christ, the victor
3. Foolish accusations

### Victory at Capernaum

1. Problems at the synagogue
2. Power of Christ
3. Pondering the truth

### Victory at Gadara

1. Christ and Legion
2. Christ and the people

### Victory at Tyre and Sidon

1. Power of Christ
2. Expression of faith

### Victory at Caesarea Philippi

1. Weakness of men
2. Power of Christ
3. Seeking for God

### Victory for Us

1. Review
2. "In Christ"
3. Discipline your life

1. The subject matter of this chapter must be handled with great wisdom. Exalt Christ and His power. Never tempt students to falter by encouraging a fascination with evil. Our job is to vaccinate the students against evil, not to infect them with it.

2. Be prepared to counsel students privately about their relationships to God. When Christ and evil are plainly contrasted, some may rightly question their relationship to God. Use the opportunity for evangelism or discipleship.

3. This subject requires significant teacher preparation in order to guide the class to the stated objectives. Do not allow discussions to wander.

4. Be bold in kindly confronting the evils of society and of the students. Confrontation is never pleasant, but neither are the consequences of sin. Introducing a young person to Christ's power will produce eternal benefits.

In theology, federal headship is the doctrine that Christ represented all men in His work and victories. See Romans 5:15-21 for a contrast between the headship of Adam and the headship of Christ.

wrestling. Reuben was greatly relieved that wrestling class was over. He just hoped that the coach would be merciful and give him a C for the semester.

Like Reuben, I had to take wrestling for a required physical education course. The coach talked a lot about being big, strong, and fast. I quickly learned that I was neither big nor strong nor fast. You can guess the results: at the time, I did not like the class at all.

In retrospect, the Lord taught me a lot through wrestling. I learned about my personal weakness in wrestling with a strong foe called *sin*. Most Christians will recognize that rebellion against God is everywhere, including inside us. All too often, we commit sin, which is just like being pinned in wrestling class. It controls and defeats us. Jesus knows about the problem. The Gospel of Mark shows us Jesus' wrestling match with the representatives of sin and gives us a strategy to defeat them.

You know from studying history or government that the president or king often acts on behalf of an entire nation. This powerful person speaks for and represents all the people. We will see Christ our leader as He fights Satan's armies that represent sin and rebellion. Jesus defeated sin, and we can too as we learn from Him. In this chapter, we will first look at Christ's explanation of the battle and then at four examples of His victory. In each case, we will see the power of Christ over evil. We will then examine the basics of a relationship with Christ that guarantees victory for us.

58

---

### Exercise: The Ten Commandments

**Goal:** To focus the students on God's law.

**Procedure:** Instruct the students to write from memory the Ten Commandments. Allow them to use a Bible after a few minutes to supplement their answers. Briefly discuss each one. Point out that the Ten Commandments reflect God's nature.

Sin is the breaking of the commandments.

### Discussion: Sin's Evidences

**Goal:** To expose sin in everyday life.

**Procedure:** Use several newspaper or periodical articles to start a discussion on how people break God's law. Ask the students to identify specific infractions. Direct the conversation toward personal failures. Invite opinions on the statement "the devil made me do

it." Point out that man is responsible for his own actions. See Romans 3:19.

## Basics of the Battle
### Mark 3:22-30

Christ's conversation with the scribes in Mark 3 occurred toward the middle of His ministry. Great crowds from all over Palestine had heard about Jesus and wanted to see Him (Mark 3:7, 8). The religious leadership in Jerusalem did not like what they were hearing and did not like the fact that so many people followed Jesus. They devised a plan to discredit His ministry, which might destroy His popularity.

To the great amazement of the crowds, Jesus cast unclean spirits, or demons, out of people. Some of the scribes came to Galilee and began to tell people that Jesus had an unclean spirit and that He cast out unclean spirits through the power of Beelzebub (Mark 3:22, 30). In order to understand this slander, let's first examine their terminology. *Unclean* means dirty or filthy. When applied to religious matters, it means that something is totally void of moral purity or value. We should also understand that the word spirit did not refer to an emotion or a personality trait. When someone enthusiastically cheers for his team, we may say that he has "spirit." But in this context, the word refers to an evil being that followed Satan in rebellion against God. While the origin of these evil beings is not certain, they are obviously evil and devoted to harming humankind.

Notice also the slanderous intent behind the scribes' use of the word *Beelzebub*. The term can mean "lord of the flies," and is associated with human and animal refuse. It may also mean "lord of the dwelling." In Jewish teaching, this evil being was the chief of the devils. The scribes wanted to associate Jesus with the emissaries of evil in order to achieve their own selfish purposes.

Jesus did not let the wicked accusations go unchallenged. His graceful response shows us the nature of the battle against evil. In Mark 3:23-26, Jesus told the scribes and the people that evil has unity of purpose and has one leader. The leader is Satan, who constantly opposes God and works against the spiritual success of mankind. His name means "adversary." Jesus reminded them that a divided kingdom or house will come to ruin. What would

Christ explains the primary issues concerning demon possession in Mark 3:22-30. That passage is treated first in order to establish a foundation for interpreting the other major sections.

Many Bible scholars believe that demon possession was not a continuous state. The Greek word for this condition could be translated "demonized." The unclean spirit took control of the person and caused destructive behavior. In some cases, the event triggered epilepsy and other medical problems.

The fact that so many cases of demon possession occurred in the first century may be due to the presence of Christ on earth. Both Jewish and secular writers attest to the phenomenon. (See the Josephus excerpt.) The appearance and activities of Satan's forces may have been an attack on Christ.

Demon possession occurs today, as many missionaries will affirm. Genuine cases in places with a Christian heritage are rare but may be increasing due to secularization and apostasy. You may need to acknowledge the possibility in class, but do not dwell on it. Turn the discussion to personal and societal evils that the students must face.

See the overhead transparency in the Appendix (p. 147) for a listing of the names of Satan in Scripture.

### Overhead: Identifying the Forces of Evil

**Goal:** To discern the character of evil in the names of Satan's forces.

**Procedure:** See the Identifying the Forces of Evil overhead in the Appendix (p. 147). Briefly go over the names of Satan and point out the evil character of each. Direct any student references to satanic activity in contemporary society back to people's responsibility for their sin.

### Exercise: The Conquering Christ

**Goal:** To consider Christ's power and majesty.

**Procedure:** Divide the class into two groups. Each group chooses one person as a representative. Using sword-drill format, read one of the verse references below. Recognize the first person who finds the verse and ask him to read it. The second group then has fifteen seconds to declare how the

verse describes Christ. The first group must decide whether the answer is correct. Assign a student to write on the board one- or two-word descriptions of Christ for each verse. A new set of students competes for each verse.

Verses

I Timothy 6:15    Potentate

Romans 11:26    Deliverer

Revelation 5:5    Lion of Judah

happen if someone on your basketball team started playing for the other side? The coach would promptly remove that person from the game and from the team. Likewise, governments execute spies for working for the enemy. Companies dismiss workers who help the competition. Jesus' words certainly imply that His actions destroy Satan's domination of men. Simply stated, Christ performed the will of God by casting out the unclean spirits and by freeing men from sin's domination. The accusation of the scribes is completely illogical even to the least educated.

Christ not only pointed out the error of scribes, He also explained His function in the battle. In Mark 3:27, notice Christ's graciousness in the story of the strong man. Jesus never said that Beelzebub is the strong man, but that is certainly the assumption based on the derivation of the name. Christ did clearly state that He is stronger than the strong man, which implies His deity. He gave the people the truth they required without exalting Himself and without needlessly offending them. Three actions characterize Christ's domination of evil. He enters the strong man's house, binds him, and then takes his possessions. Christ entered the domain of evil at His birth and more particularly when His public ministry began. Christ also silenced and controlled the unclean spirits, which points to their binding. The fact that Jesus freed people from unclean spirits indicates the

The life of Christ is characterized by the battle with Satan and evil. Direct attacks by Satan recorded in the Gospels occurred in Herod's slaughter of the infants in Matthew 2:16-18, at the temptation of Christ, and then at the events surrounding the cross. The examples of demon exorcism were minor skirmishes compared to Christ's victory over death at the Resurrection. Christ controlled Satan and his evil allies at every battle. Such control serves to highlight Christ's willing humiliation at the cross.

Acts 10:36   Lord

Isaiah 9:6   Mighty God, Prince of Peace

Hebrews 2:10   Captain of salvation

Acts 3:15   Prince of life

spoiling of Satan's possessions. The matchless power of Christ defeats even the worst examples of evil.

One additional thought must also be noted. The scribes accused Jesus of unthinkable evil. Jesus kindly refuted them. He then pointed out the seriousness of their sin before God.

## Flavius Josephus: Jewish Historian

Josephus (A.D. 37-100) spent his early years studying Jewish religion. He later traveled to Rome to ask Nero for the freedom of two priests. While there, he learned about the Roman government and way of life. After returning to Palestine, he supported Jewish freedom fighters and saw the destruction of Herod's temple. A military commander then sent Josephus to Rome as a prisoner. Once released, he wrote several large books detailing the history of the Jews for the benefit of the Romans. The following excerpt shows a Jewish remedy that uses a tree root to cure demon possession.

"There is a certain place called Baaras, which produces a root of the same name with itself; its colour is like to that of flame, and towards the evening it sends out a certain ray like lightning: it is not easily taken by such as would do it, but recedes from their hands, nor will yield itself to be taken quietly. They dig a trench quite around it, till the hidden part be very small, then they tie a dog to it, and when the dog tries hard to follow him that tied him, this root is easily plucked up, but the dog dies immediately, as if it were instead the man that would take the plant away. Yet, after all this pains in getting it, it is only valuable on account of one virtue it hath, that if it be brought to sick persons, it quickly drives away those called Demons, which are no other than the spirits of the wicked, which enter into men that are alive, and kill them, unless they can obtain some help against them" (Josephus, *Wars of the Jews*, Book 7, Chapter 6, paragraph 3).

Many theologians do not believe that modern man can commit the sin of the scribes as recorded in Mark 3:28, 29. Man cannot see the works of Christ, as did these scribes, and therefore, the sin may not be committed. Pastors and counselors often report dealing with people who worry that they have committed the "unpardonable sin." Romans 5:20 provides great encouragement to those who are swallowed up in sin.

Attributing Christ's power to an evil spirit, or blasphemy against the Holy Spirit, is a sin so heinous that God will not forgive it. Jesus implied that these seemingly righteous men had no fellowship with God. By rejecting Christ, they cut themselves off from the source of true life and are now swallowed up in the realm of evil.

Some people worry that they may have committed this sin. There is no need for God's children to worry. At the heart of blasphemy against the Holy Spirit is a total hatred of God. Because those who worry about this sin show tenderness for the things of God, they have certainly not committed the unpardonable sin.

## Victory at Capernaum
### Mark 1:23-28

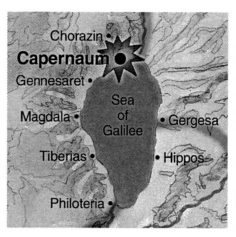

Jesus' great preaching ministry brought Him to the synagogue at Capernaum. The people wondered at His teaching because it was so unlike the contradictory doctrines of the religious leaders. Mark tells us that the congregation included a man with an unclean spirit. The very fact that such a person would attend Sabbath services pointed to the deadness of the people's religion and understanding.

Perhaps they did not recognize the man's true problem, or they may have lacked the power to do anything about it. The man with the unclean spirit immediately recognized Jesus and exclaimed, "What have we to do with thee?" The literal Greek translation is "what to us and to you," meaning that the two parties have nothing in common. The evil spirit thinks that Jesus came from Nazareth to Capernaum to ruin him. As the Holy One of God, Jesus' control of the unclean spirit was absolute.

62

See Deuteronomy 25:4 about muzzling an animal.

Swete suggests that Christ enforced silence upon the unclean spirit because a holy God will accept praise only from a holy being. Second, the demon's invasion of the man is outside the natural order (Swete, 20).

Emphasizing the superiority of a faith-based relationship to Christ over religious experience may be new to some students. Many seemingly good religious events invigorate the emotions and create feelings of good will, but these do not equal a relationship to Christ. Faithful obedience to the Word of God is the path to God. See Peter's comments about the experience on the mount of transfiguration compared to the effect of God's Word in II Peter 1:16-21.

## Discussion: Soda Can Experiences

**Goal:** To illustrate the difference between an experience and a relationship.

**Procedure:** Bring a can of soda to the class and ask someone to drink it. Allow the class to ask the person various questions about drinking the soda. In most cases, the student will talk about the product and not about the can. Explain that the can simply brought the soda to the person and that the can has minimal value. The drink is now a part of the student. So Christ should become a part of us. The experience brings the relationship.

Use whatever is available for similar object lessons. A water fountain works well. We appreciate the water and think little of the means of getting the water.

Mark tells us that Jesus rebuked him. The term *rebuke* points to Jesus' superiority over the unclean spirit. A school principal may rebuke a student for poor grades, but a student would never rebuke a principal. Two things about the unclean spirit must change. First, he must hold his peace or be quiet. The Greek verb literally means "be muzzled." Just as a pet owner puts a muzzle onto a dog to keep it from biting or barking, so Christ silenced any testimony about Himself from the unclean spirit. Only holy beings have the liberty to publicly exalt a holy God. He also told the spirit to come out of the man. The power and nature of Christ compelled the spirit to obey. The man's convulsions and cry proved to the onlookers that the unclean spirit actually departed.

The people in the synagogue reacted with utter amazement at Jesus' power. The religious leaders performed elaborate ceremonies and prescribed medicines to remove demons. Jesus was something new. Evidently, intense discussions broke out about the events in the synagogue. News spread quickly throughout the region. Just who was this man, and how could he have such great power? We know that this man was God's Son, the Messiah of Israel. Mark begins his Gospel with a simple declaration about Christ's person and then proceeds to show us the events that prove Jesus' claims of deity. Christians trust all that Jesus said and did. But we know from Mark that many of the people who saw and heard Jesus never really believed him. They instead wondered and talked about Him. Most seemed glad for the benefits of healing and for the removal of unclean spirits, but they never repented and trusted. Experiences must lead to Christ. Real victory over evil in our lives begins when we move beyond the experience and into a trusting relationship with Christ.

## Discussion: Religious Experiences

**Goal:** To evaluate religious experience against faith.

**Procedure:** Emphasize to the class that God requires faith for salvation and growth. Experiences have spiritual value only as they lead to a solid relationship with Christ. Ask the class to state how typical teen activities can lead to a relationship with Christ or may be just another good time. A good example is music. Some modern religious music does little more than excite the emotions and provide entertainment. On the other hand, music that exalts Christ can lead to a life-changing relationship with the Lord. The differences in some cases are subtle, but very real.

## Victory at Gadara
### Mark 5:1-20

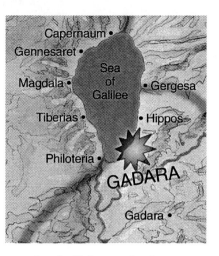

Jesus' next major battle with evil took place on the Sea of Galilee's east bank in the region known as Gadara. The Romans built ten Greek-style cities in the area. The new Roman and Greek culture attracted many Jews who retained their Jewish nationality but who also enjoyed the corrupt pagan practices and prosperity. Most Jews from Judea despised these people for their relationship to the Romans. The strange mix of religions and cultures made a great place for Jesus to teach us about Himself and His power.

We can only imagine what the disciples thought as they stepped off the boat onto the shore of this wicked place and saw a demon-possessed man running toward them from the tombs. Mark's detailed description of the man probably reflects Peter's fear. But notice this man's subjection to Jesus in Mark 5:6, 7. He ran to Jesus, worshiped Him, and then begged Him for a reprieve from torment. Jesus asked the demon's name for the benefit of the disciples. A legion was a powerful, well-equipped army of about six thousand Roman soldiers. The emperor used many legions to conquer the world and to maintain control over unruly provinces like Judea. Jesus stood face to face with a great army of demons and, by simply speaking, He cast them out of the man. The demons asked Jesus to allow them to enter a herd of hogs that were feeding near the mountains. Old Testament law prohibited the Jews from eating pork and so it's possible that the owners of the pigs were disobedient Jews. Jesus granted their request to prove that He had removed the demons from the man and to prick

64

### Worksheet: Christ's Transforming Power

**Goal:** To develop Bible study skills and expose the misery of sin.

**Procedure:** See the Christ's Transforming Power worksheet in the Appendix (pp. 148-49). Each student should individually complete the worksheet for a grade. Emphasize the misery of sin.

the conscience of the Jews in the area. When the demons entered the animals, they immediately ran over a cliff, fell into the sea, and were drowned. Even in a hostile place when confronted by hordes of unclean spirits, the Son of God demonstrated His power over evil and His compassion for man.

The next skirmish in the battle shows us two very different reactions to Christ's power. Like messengers at a battle, the pig keepers ran through the region and reported the news to everyone. The crowd came and saw not only Jesus, but also the man who was now perfectly normal. Mark tells us that the people reacted with fear and wanted Jesus to leave. Ancient pagans often feared unknown spiritual powers. Jesus represented a threat to their religion. Or maybe they were upset about the economic consequences of losing the pigs.

In either case, they preferred to be left alone, and Jesus departed from them. Observe now the request of the man who had been freed from the demons. He wanted to be with Jesus. Christ announced different plans for this man. Since the people had rejected Christ's personal ministry to them, He would now send one of their own to testify of the truth. The man obediently departed and told everyone about Jesus' power and compassion. These responses near the Sea of Galilee occur all over the world today. Some will reject Christ for various reasons. Others will obediently believe Him. We can evaluate our personal relationship to God based on our response to Christ's power and compassion.

65

Mark 5:15 shows the power of Christ to restore depraved humans. The man was sitting as opposed to running, which indicates a restful soul. He was clothed and not naked, which indicates proper modesty. He was in his right mind, which indicates a renewed ability to think and to function properly.

Rejection of Christ results in His departure, which is an evidence of judgment. Notice however that Christ sent the man back to his own people to witness to them. Even when rejected, Christ left a messenger to spread the news of His grace, thereby giving the people of Gadara another opportunity to believe.

In Mark 5:19, Jesus calls Himself "Lord."

## Overhead: The Battlefields

**Goal:** To teach basic Bible geography and to illustrate Christ's work among all people groups.

**Procedure:** Show the Battlefields overhead from the Appendix (p. 150). Point out the variety of places and people groups involved when Jesus cast out unclean spirits. Some people affirm that Christianity is only for one race or nationality. Emphasize that location or culture does not limit Christ's power.

## Victory at Tyre and Sidon
### Mark 7:24-30

See I Kings 17 for the story of Elijah and the widow.

The word translated "dogs" is actually a diminutive form in Greek meaning "little dogs." Vicious packs of dogs roamed Palestine's villages, but the animal referred to by Christ was a small household pet.

Christ's reference to the woman as a dog should be taken to denote her status as a Gentile. The general character of Christ's statement to the woman seems much stronger in English than is indicated by the Greek grammar and by the culture of the day. However, Christ clearly communicates that Israel was His main priority. His actions show that the Gentile may share in the blessings. See Romans 11 for Paul's analysis.

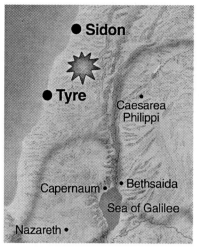

After Jesus finished rebuking the religious leaders, He decided to travel toward Tyre and Sidon. He probably wanted to get away from Galilee in order to teach the disciples in private and to get some rest. These two well-known Roman seaports were infused with Gentile culture. Elijah had stayed with a widow and her son in this area, and God miraculously sustained them with meal and oil for a long time. In this spiritually dark place, Jesus showed His power over evil and showed the surprising faith of a Gentile woman.

Jesus quietly entered a house, but Mark 7:25 records that somehow, a Gentile woman whose daughter had an unclean spirit knew about Jesus and found Him at the house. In typical oriental fashion, she fell at His feet, signifying submission, and asked Jesus to cast out her daughter's unclean spirit. The fact that the daughter was in another location points to the woman's great faith. Jesus then acted to further expose her faith for our encouragement. "Let the children first be filled: for it is not meet to take the children's bread and cast it unto the dogs" reflected a common household scene. Small pet dogs sat under the kitchen table looking for scraps or crumbs that fell to the floor. Jesus gently reminded her that His ministry was primarily to the Jews and that her lowly position as a Gentile did not entitle her to the request. The woman's wise response

66

---

## Exercise: Gentile Promises

**Goal:** To review the Bible's teaching about salvation for the Gentiles.

**Procedure:** Divide the class into several groups. Write the verses listed below on the board. Instruct the groups to look up each verse and determine the theme that binds the verses together. The first group to accurately write the theme on paper and give it to the instructor should be recognized or rewarded in some way.

Once all groups have responded, review the basic content of the verses.

Verses: Genesis 12:3; Psalm 22:27; Isaiah 45:22, 23; 60:3; Malachi 1:11; Matthew 12:18. (Many others could also be used.)

Theme: God's promises to the Gentiles, or salvation for the Gentiles.

acknowledged Jesus' mission to the Jews, but pointed out that Christ's abundance was plenty for all. Jesus rewarded her faith by granting the request. He completely removed the unclean spirit from the daughter, which brought about a state of rest for both the mother and the girl. The mother's persistent and wise faith enabled Christ to display His power and compassion.

## Spiritual Warfare

**PRINCIPLES APPLIED**

John Bunyan (1628-1688) spent about twelve years in an English prison for preaching the gospel of Christ. The prison cell restricted his movements but could not restrict his zeal for God. Bunyan wrote *The Pilgrim's Progress*, an allegorical story about the Christian life, as well as eleven other books. The following selection chronicles Christian's battle with Apollyon, the evil ruler of this world. Notice the weapon Christian uses to defeat his enemy.

Then Apollyon, espying his opportunity, began to gather up close to Christian, and wrestling with him, gave him a dreadful fall; and with that, Christian's sword flew out of his hand. Then said Apollyon, I am sure of thee now. And with that he had almost pressed him to death; so that Christian began to despair of life: but as God would have it, while Apollyon was fetching of his last blow, thereby to make a full end of this good man, Christian nimbly stretched out his hand for his sword, and caught it, saying, "Rejoice not against me, O mine enemy: when I fall, I shall arise" (Micah 7:8); and with that gave him a deadly thrust, which made him give back, as one that had received his mortal wound. Christian perceiving that, made at him again, saying, "Nay, in all these things we are more than conquerors through Him that loved us" (Rom. 8:37).

And with that Apollyon spread forth his dragon's wings, and sped him away, that Christian for a season saw him no more (James 4:7).

Some students may be unfamiliar with *The Pilgrim's Progress* and with the sword as a symbol of God's Word. See Ephesians 6:17. See the Internet or encyclopedias for information about John Bunyan. His life is an excellent example of Christ's power to save a hardened sinner and to sustain people through difficult circumstances.

## Exercise: *The Pilgrim's Progress*

**Goal:** To expose the students to good literature.

**Procedure:** Obtain *The Pilgrim's Progress* from a library or bookstore. Read one or more of the sections about Christian's struggle with sin and evil. As an alternative, obtain a recording of the book and listen to a selected section. Emphasize the universal nature of struggle with sin and the victory found in Christ.

## Victory at Caesarea Philippi
### Mark 9:14-29

Caesarea Philippi was the home of the Roman governor of Palestine. The transfiguration of Christ and other events of Mark 9 took place near, but not in, this city.

In this case, the unclean spirit seems to have caused epilepsy in the boy.

As with other victims of demon possession, Christ did not expect the boy to exercise faith. The actual lesson about faith revolved around the father and his struggles. Christ's play on the father's words in Mark 9:23 reinforced the need for a strong and mature faith. Once Christ cured the father's faith problem, He could help the boy. A lesson exists here for parents. Many problems with children stem from parental failure. When the parent receives help, the child's problems disappear.

In Mark 9:29, the KJV and NKJV have "prayer *and fasting.*" Fasting (planned abstinence from food) does not in itself please God. Christ taught that it is an act of personal devotion, not a public display or a token of spirituality, as many today want to make it. See Matthew 6:16-18.

Jesus had just returned with Peter, James, and John from the mountain of transfiguration. Any doubts about Christ's deity should have been settled for the three disciples. They had seen Jesus in His glory and heard the affirming voice of God the Father about His Son. Upon entering an area around the city, they saw and heard the scribes interrogating the disciples about their

inability to cast out an unclean spirit from a boy. It's ironic that the scribes who could not help this man and his son would question someone else for trying. Jesus asked them about the debate, and the father related the boy's condition. Again we see Christ's unchallenged power. At the appropriate moment, He simply commanded the spirit to depart and ministered to the boy's remaining

weakness. What the disciples could not do, Jesus accomplished with ease. God's power always vanquishes evil.

Jesus used this event to teach both the father and the disciples several important lessons. Let's consider the father's situation first. The fact that he was desperate for help is obvious from the long description of his son's affliction. Jesus invited the father to tell Him even more by asking when the problem had started. The father answered with more information and with a plea. "But

68

if thou canst do any thing, have compassion on us, and help us" shows faith, but the faith needs to mature. He questioned the power of Christ instead of acknowledging his own deficiency. Jesus exposed the real issue with His answer. He used the father's own words to show him the need for strong faith. When the father confessed his weakness, Jesus granted the request. The healed son would constantly remind the father of two vital principles: sinful man is weak and Christ is strong and compassionate.

Secondly, Jesus had a lesson for the disciples. He rebuked the crowd, and the disciples in particular, by calling them a "faithless generation." After the son was restored, the disciples asked Jesus why they could not cast out the unclean spirit. Jesus told them that this situation required a close relationship with God cultivated through prayer and fasting. Some situations are humanly more difficult than others. The disciples could handle the tough problems only as they drew closer to God. Notice, however, that the words of Christ crushed the most difficult problems with evil.

## Victory for Us

Mark gives us four detailed accounts in which Jesus defeated the representatives of sin and showed great compassion for man. The locations and circumstances differed, but the power of Christ was always the same. Jesus displayed His power and authority to teach us important spiritual lessons. Some wondered at His power but never really believed. Others asked Jesus to depart, and He granted their shortsighted request. But Jesus acted to strengthen the faith of those who truly believed. They enjoyed the freedom and victory of knowing the Son of God.

You are probably very familiar with the story of David and Goliath. The Philistine giant wanted to fight the champion of

See I Samuel 17 for the story of David and Goliath.

69

---

### Discussion: Faith Builders

**Goal:** To provide simple steps to increasing personal faith.

**Procedure:** Ask the students to state to the class how teens can strengthen their faith. Direct the discussion to the verses listed below. Emphasize that a growing faith requires daily decisions that any teen can make. Later in the week or in the course, ask the students what they are doing to increase their faith.

Romans 10:17  Study the Bible.

Hebrews 5:14  Act on what you know.

Hebrews 10:25  Attend church and other spiritually refreshing activities.

Israel to determine the winner of the war between the two countries. Goliath's size and strength scared even the most experienced soldiers of Israel. One day, David heard the giant's threats and blasphemies. The young shepherd boy found some smooth stones and used his sling to hurl one of them right between the giant's eyes. Goliath died at David's hand. The Israelites chased and defeated the Philistine armies. Just as David, the representative of Israel, defeated the giant, so Christ our representative defeated the powers of evil when He cast out unclean spirits.

The Apostle Paul writes often about believers being "in Christ," which seems to be a difficult concept to understand. But, from the Gospel of Mark, we see that Christ defeated Satan at every battle. My biggest problem is not physical health, mental weakness, lack of money, or other people. The inward struggle with my sinful heart is my most difficult and persistent problem. If you have trusted Christ as your Savior, you have the same struggles. Being "in Christ" means that He has won the victory over evil for me. I cannot do it for myself. Only the all-powerful Son of God can defeat the enemy of my soul. My part is to believe that I win through Jesus and then to chase the enemies out of my heart. Most of us will have doubts and fears about God's dealings in our lives from time to time. The best weapon against such assaults is to remember God's goodness to us in the past and then to find His comforting promises to us in the Bible. Modern technology continually presents evil to us through television, newspapers, radio, and the Internet. We may need to guard our hearts by avoiding or restricting these conduits of rebellion against God. We will never completely win the battle against wickedness in this world. Mark 16:19 tells us that Christ "was received up into heaven, and sat on the right hand of God." Because believers are in Christ, one day we too will sit with Christ in heaven, far away from the pollution of this evil world. I look forward to that day and hope that you do as well.

Paul uses the phrase "in Christ" about seventy-four times to describe the relationship between the Savior and the redeemed.

Just as the knowledge of our personal sinfulness pointed us to Christ for cleansing, so our continued struggle with sin motivates us to stay close to Christ. The daily fight with sin is a good indication of genuine salvation. Those who have no awareness of sin may still be spiritually dead. See I John 1:5-10.

## Discussion: Teen Struggles

**Goal:** To aid teens in the struggle against sin.

**Procedures:** Midway through the chapter's lessons, ask the students to write down and turn in a short list of things that influence them toward evil. Choose the most common responses. Prepare a short help seminar for later in the teaching sequence on each issue. Show the students how God's Word can guide them and how they must decide to follow God's ways if they desire victory over evil. Encourage them to meditate on Christ's victory.

## Roman Armor and Christian Battle

The apostle Paul sat in a Roman prison chained to a soldier. Probably as a result of Julius Caesar's murder, the Roman emperors had decided to keep the best legions close to the capital for protection. The soldier's armor inspired Paul's thoughts about the believer's warfare with evil. Believers today can stand against every type of evil by using the Christian soldier's armor. Are you prepared for the battle?

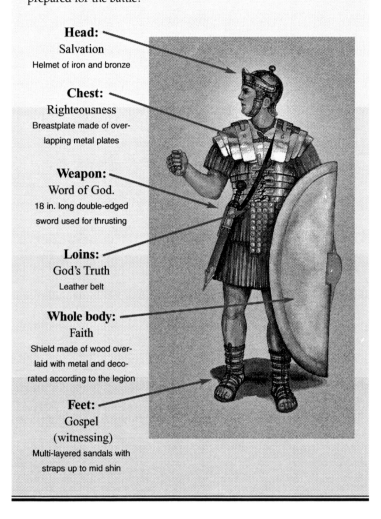

**Head:**
Salvation
Helmet of iron and bronze

**Chest:**
Righteousness
Breastplate made of over-
lapping metal plates

**Weapon:**
Word of God.
18 in. long double-edged
sword used for thrusting

**Loins:**
God's Truth
Leather belt

**Whole body:**
Faith
Shield made of wood over-
laid with metal and deco-
rated according to the legion

**Feet:**
Gospel
(witnessing)
Multi-layered sandals with
straps up to mid shin

The following verses relate to Paul's description of the Christian's armor.

Truth: John 1:17; 14:6.

Righteousness: Matthew 5:6; Roman 4:3

Witnessing: Matthew 28:19, 20; I Corinthians 15:3, 4.

Faith: Romans 1:17; Ephesians 2:8, 9.

Salvation: Acts 16:31; I John 5:4.

Word of God: Psalm 119:9; Hebrews 4:12.

# Review Questions

1. What religious group opposed Christ's ministry in Galilee?

   **Scribes**

2. Give one of the two possible meanings of *Beelzebub.*

   **Lord of the flies or lord of the dwelling**

3. What does Satan's name mean?

   **Adversary**

4. Who took the strong man's possessions in Mark 3?

   **Jesus**

5. What is the literal meaning of *hold your peace?*

   **"Be muzzled"**

6. Who wrote a history of the Jews?

   **Josephus**

7. What is the name of a large Roman army?

   **Legion**

8. Who fought with Christian in Pilgrim's Progress?

   *Apollyon*


9. What Gentile seaport towns did Jesus travel near?

   *Tyre and Sidon*


10. What weapon does the Christian soldier use?

    *Sword of the Spirit or the Word of God*


11. What did Jesus call His disciples and the crowd at Caesarea?

    *Faithless generation*


12. What did Jesus want the father in Caesarea to confess?

    *His personal weakness*


## Essay

13. What did Jesus do to cast out unclean spirits?

*He spoke or commanded them to depart.*

73

14. Contrast Jesus' method of casting out unclean spirits with the Jews' methods.

*The Jews used medicines and elaborate ceremonies, which were largely ineffective. Jesus simply spoke and the demons departed.*

15. Why did the hogs run into the sea?

*Unclean spirits entered them.*

16. How did unclean spirits show subjection to Christ?

*They acknowledged His person and obeyed His word.*

17. Why were the disciples powerless to remove the unclean spirit near Caesarea?

*The disciples lacked faith. Jesus told them to pray and fast in difficult cases in order to have the power of God.*

18. Why did Jesus send the man who had been possessed by the legion back to his own country?

*The people asked Jesus to leave. In order to maintain a witness to those people, He sent the man back to tell everyone about Jesus' power.*

19. How did the woman near Tyre show submission to Christ?

*She fell at His feet.*

20. What is the meaning of "in Christ"?

*"In Christ" means that all the benefits and blessings of Christ's victory can be mine. I cannot win by myself. Christ won for me.*

75

# CHAPTER FIVE

# Christ and the Religious Leadership
5

Adam Nelson's and David Cummings's hearts raced faster as the bottom of the inning started. David hardly noticed his wet and sticky shirt. Their high school team, the Winchester Cougars, had tied the final game of the regular season with a home run in the last inning. They needed to keep the other team from scoring in order to put the game into extra innings.

Adam yelled, "I guess I need to buy you a soft drink since I knocked yours out of your hand and onto your shirt. I got a little excited when the ball flew over the fence!"

"If we win this game, I'll buy you a super-sized milk shake for putting up with all my cheering and screaming," answered David.

The first batter came to the plate and promptly struck out. Both guys jumped up and shouted approvingly to the team. They quickly sat down when the next guy hit a long double into right field. After walking the next batter, the pitcher looked tired, so the coach immediately brought in Phil Larson to finish the game. Phil had a perfect pitching record of four wins and no losses. He was the best man for the job. Adam and David started shouting along with the rest of the fans from Winchester.

Phil's first pitch was hit directly at the short stop for an easy second out. The next pitch hit the batter to load the bases. David

77

## Lecture Overview

### Introduction

1. Life's disappointments
2. Basics of Christ's conflict with religion
3. Religious groups in the NT

### The Period of Curiosity

1. Forgiving sins
2. Associating with sinners
3. Conforming to tradition
4. Observing the Sabbath

### Conspiracy Against Christ

1. Traditions
2. Exploitation
3. Authority
4. Government control
5. Resurrection
6. Greatest commandment
7. Lordship of Messiah

### Condemnation of Christ

1. Trial
2. Resurrection

### Final Thoughts

1. Review Mark's record
2. Applications for today

### Thoughts for the Teacher

1. Chapter 5 deals with a subject that is contrary to society's philosophy. Post-modernism teaches that all ideas are equal: absolutes do not exist. But Christ acted upon the absolute authority of God's Word in condemning false religious practice.

2. Many students will have little or no background in dealing with conflicting ideas and philosophies. This chapter will expose the student to man-oriented religion. Exalt the Word of God as the sole authority for evaluating these issues. Be bold but kind when discussing modern religious practice. Our beliefs have eternal consequences.

3. Space does not permit the treatment of each section of Mark's Gospel. A worksheet is provided to develop an overview of this issue. It will also encourage good Bible study skills.

4. Maintain the emphasis on reading the text of Mark. See the Appendix (p. 134) for ideas to keep the exercise fresh. Remember that the goal of the course is to infuse the student with the Word of God.

Many people use the failures of others as an excuse to ignore their responsibility to God. These people will generally delight in talking about the sins of others. Romans 2:2; 3:19; and 3:23 will focus the attention on the real problem, which is every man's relationship to God.

said that the ball was supposed to curve, but for some reason it had not. Both guys seemed to have absolute confidence in Phil's pitching. After a brief conference between pitcher and catcher, the game resumed. Phil threw two quick strikes, and everybody stood to cheer. The next pitch flew over the catcher's head and hit the backstop! The game promptly ended when the runner at third base jogged home for the winning run.

As the guys walked out of the stadium, Adam mumbled, "This is absolutely my last baseball game."

David reassured him, "Don't be so gloomy! Everyone fails at one time or another. The whole team will play again next year, and we have a great shot at winning the state championship."

Adam shrugged his shoulders and walked quietly to the car. The guys did enjoy two very large milk shakes, and they laughed about the wet shirt. Neither said a word about baseball. It would be ten years before Adam would attend another game.

Most of us regularly deal with disappointments of one type or another. The death of a family member, a poor grade in a hard class, or the loss of a ball game can lead to emotional distress. One of the hardest situations for us to handle appropriately is improper behavior by religious leaders. We perceive that something is wrong, and then

78

## Worksheet: Christ Deals with the Religious Leadership

**Goal:** To comprehend the basic facts of Christ's conflict with the religious leaders.

**Procedure:** See the Christ Deals with the Religious Leadership worksheet in the Appendix (pp. 151-54). Allow the students to use their Bibles to fill out the chart. Consider using the exercise for homework or as a group project. Grade the work for completeness.

# Important Information To Keep On Your Fridge

## Prices
Early Bird Special Before 8/27
$65
**Regular Price**
$85
**Transportation**
$25

## Transportation
This year we will not be providing transportation since our destination is much closer than before. However, we will be making the church bus available for students for a cost of $25 for transport on Saturday morning and Sunday afternoon. The bus will leave EBC Student Center at 7:30 am on Saturday and will return students at 5:30 pm on Sunday. You must call 770-971-2323 x136 and reserve a spot as there are only 24 available.

**IMPORTANT MEDICAL INFORMATION: WE NEED NEW MEDICAL /PERMISSION FORMS FOR THE 06/07 YEAR. PLEASE COMPLETE BOTH ENCLOSED FORMS AND ATTACH A COPY OF YOUR MEDICAL CARD WITH YOUR REGISTRATION.**

### Emergency Numbers
Patrick: 770-401-0619
WinShape: 706-238-7714
Or
706-238-7733

### To Bring List
Bible
Modest Casual Clothes
Sleeping Bag/Linens/Pillow
Toiletries (soap, towel, etc.)
Flashlight
Snack or Drinks to Share
NO SANDALS

#### Not To Bring
Electronics, valuables, fireworks, tobacco, non-prescription drugs, alcohol

### Schedule
Saturday 9 am  Registration
(Breakfast will not be served)
Morning Session
Lunch
Afternoon Rec/Team Building
Dinner
Evening Session
Sunday         Morning Session
Lunch
2 pm  Parents Join Praise/Worship
4 pm  Dismissal

Parents: Don't miss the opportunity to join your student during Praise/Worship Sunday afternoon from 2-4 pm.

## Directions to WinShape Wilderness

**From Atlanta:**
* Approximate driving time: 1 hour 20 minutes.
* Take I-75 North to exit 290 (Rome-Canton).
* Turn left off of exit ramp and follow road until it ends at a traffic light, approximately 2 miles.
* At the traffic light, turn left and then make an *immediate* right towards HWY 411-20.
* Travel 2.9 miles (through 4 traffic lights) and exit to the right HWY 411-20 (Rome).
* Travel on HWY 411-20 for approximately 16 miles to the east Rome bypass (Rome 1).
* Turn right onto Rome 1 at the traffic light with a Shell station on the left.
* Continue for 10 miles on Rome 1; at the 6th traffic light turn right onto HWY 27 (Martha Berry Blvd.)
* At the 1st traffic light, turn left into the main entrance of Berry College.
* ***Note: follow your map to the Winshape Center or stop at the gatehouse for a map to mountain campus.**

***To WinShape Centre From Entrance to Berry College:*** *Once you have entered the main gate of Berry College, continue forward to the round-about driveway and circle right. Take the second right placing you on the right side of Hermann Hall and continue to the stop sign. Take a right and go to next stop sign. Take a left and continue down the stretch road approximately three miles until you hit a speed bump. The Centre is straight ahead of you. This is where you will need to check in.*

like Adam we decide to abandon everything related to the situation.

The consequences of such a decision can destroy our lives for both time and eternity. Others of us will maintain a respect for God, but will shun church and any contact with Christians out of the fear of being disappointed again. These people may know Christ as their Savior, but they fail to enjoy the life that God has planned for them. One of the big obstacles to Christian maturity is learning to recognize and deal with religious hypocrites and failures.

Even a cursory reading of Mark's Gospel reveals that Jesus often exposed the sin and weakness of the religious leadership in Israel. The common people gladly received Christ's teaching. Did these people realize that something was wrong with their leaders? Christ's words and actions attracted great multitudes because they saw in Jesus something better and something new. As deity, Jesus had the right to judge the deeds of a religion that supposedly pointed people to God. He also had the ability to explain God's Word so that people might repent and believe.

The religion of the day was man-oriented and failed to meet God's standards. Most of the leaders looked at Jesus as a threat to their way of life. In Mark 11:28, they asked Him, "By what authority doest thou these things? and who gave thee this authority to do these things?" They saw Christ's great power, but failed to understand His deity and His authority. Jesus' evaluation of these people is simple. At the end of His time on earth, Jesus told the disciples that "the Son of man is betrayed into the hands of sinners" (Mark 14:41). The "sinners" included the religious leaders in Jerusalem. Jesus did not let the failures and hostility of popular religion stop Him from doing the will of God. Neither should we. Mark presents to us the religious leadership's three different approaches to dealing with Christ. Each one reveals the superiority of knowing Christ personally over participating in failed religion. Understanding both the greatness of Christ and the foolishness of man's religion will insulate us from disappointments, which are certain to come.

Modern Bible believers face opposition from two groups: non-Christian religious people and nominal Christians who disbelieve the Bible.

Pagan religious practices and influence continue to increase in the western world. Many traditionally Christian groups have abandoned their faith and embraced secular philosophy while keeping outward ritual. The best way to discern all false religion is to know the source of truth and life, the Lord Jesus Christ. Detailed scrutiny of false religion must not replace the study of Christ.

79

## Discussion: Bad Guys in the Bible

**Goal:** To reinforce the reality of weak or evil people in religion throughout time.

**Procedure:** Write the names listed below on the chalkboard or overhead. Ask the students to tell you what they associate with each person. Use the verses as needed to prompt correct answers. At the end of the discussion, summarize the facts and remind the students of the need to deal with religious failures.

Aaron    Exodus 32

Demas    II Timothy 4:10

Eli    I Samuel 2

Jeroboam    I Kings 14

Judas    Mark 14

Lot    Genesis 13

Simon the Sorcerer    Acts 8

See Bible encyclopedias or the Internet for additional information about the various Jewish groups.

## Jewish Religious Groups of the First Century

Religious practices can be very confusing to people of differing times and cultures. Mark needed to explain even to the Romans the hand-washing rituals of the Pharisees. (See Mark 7:3, 4.) Background knowledge about Jewish religious practices and organizations will greatly enhance our understanding of the Gospels.

Pharisees: The Pharisees first organized about 150 B.C. as a reaction against heathen practices. Their name means "separate ones." According to Josephus, who was a Pharisee, the group had about six thousand members at the time of Christ. They believed the Old Testament law plus many oral traditions from rabbis through the years. Jesus rejected the oral traditions because they were merely the teachings of man. Strict separation from all pagan and heathen influence motivated many of the Pharisees' practices. Following the destruction of Jerusalem in A.D. 70, the Pharisees established a settlement near the Mediterranean Sea. Over the centuries Phariseeism developed into modern Orthodox Judaism.

Sadducees: The politically astute Sadducees were primarily upper-class priests who controlled temple worship and civil government. They believed in only the five books of Moses and rejected the Pharisees' oral traditions. Most did not believe in the resurrection or in anything supernatural. The Sadducees maintained their power by cooperating with the Romans. Most took Greek names. They ceased to exist as a group once the temple was destroyed.

### The Period of Curiosity
#### Mark 2:1–3:6

This section records five separate confrontations between Christ and representatives from various religious groups. The conflict escalates from internal reasoning about Christ's actions (Mark 2:6) to questioning Jesus' disciples (Mark 2:16), to confronting Jesus about the actions of the disciples (Mark 2:24), and finally to plotting to kill Jesus (Mark 3:6). The scribes and Pharisees seemed to watch Jesus' every move. They wanted to learn more about Him, which seems very commendable on the surface. Jesus pointed out their weaknesses so that they might repent and believe. Regrettably, these men did not understand because they held onto religious tradition and practice.

80

### Exercise: Headlines from the Sermon on the Mount

**Goal:** To evaluate the Sermon on the Mount for teaching on religious problems.

**Procedure:** Assign the reading of Matthew 5-7 and look for Christ's teaching on religious practices. Divide the class into several groups. Instruct the students to formulate one or two newspaper headlines from each chapter about Christ's teaching on religion.

Have the students write them on the board. Choose the best headlines by vote of the class. Make specific applications to the students based on the teaching.

Herodians: The Herodians are not known outside the New Testament. Their name suggests that the group was closely associated with King Herod. They may have believed that Herod was the best hope for a free Israel.

Essenes: The Essenes are not directly mentioned in the Gospels; however, Josephus and other historians attest to their existence. They withdrew from Jewish society in order to wait for the Messiah and to preserve the purity of their beliefs. Some archeologists believe that the Essenes had a village near Jerusalem and that Jesus entered the village to eat the Last Supper with His disciples.

Scribes: The scribes were not a political movement, but rather experts on the law. Many Pharisees were scribes. They made copies of the law and acted as the secretaries in meetings of the Sanhedrin.

Sanhedrin: The Sanhedrin was a governmental body of about seventy men who controlled Jewish political and religious affairs. In Christ's time, the high priest acted as president of the group. Most members were from wealthy families and included scribes and Sadducees. King Herod evidently favored the Pharisees and gave them seats on the council. This body tried and condemned Jesus. (See Mark 14:55 and 15:1.)

Many of you are familiar with the events in Mark 2:1-12. Four men carried a sick friend to Jesus. Since they could not come inside the house, they decided to go up to the roof, remove a section of it, and then lower their friend into Jesus' presence for healing.

Christ did heal this man, but more importantly, He taught us some important lessons about Himself. Mark records that faith reveals the power of God (Mark 2:5). The scribes looked to ritual and to traditional teachings for a relationship to God. Jesus first dealt with the sick man's sin, which was his most critical need. Perhaps the man feared that his personal sin caused the physical impairment. Maybe he had heard Jesus preaching about repentance and realized that he was a sinner like everyone else. The scribes reasoned correctly that only God could forgive sins, but they did not recognize that Jesus was God. Jesus gave them an

The houses in most Jewish villages were very close together for security. Most also had flat roofs. The four men could have easily walked from one roof to the next in order to get to the house where Jesus taught.

For God's prerogative to forgive sin, see Exodus 34:6, 7; Numbers 14; Psalm 25:7; and many others.

81

## Discussion: Outcasts from Society

**Goal:** To encourage Christlike compassion.

**Procedure:** Ask the students to list types of people who are outcasts from the local community. Write the information on the board or overhead and ask the students why these people are outcasts. Direct the discussion toward what Christ would do for these people.

Emphasize the need for faith and repentance.

Many people either had two names or took new names following major events in their lives. Examples include Abram (Abraham), Jacob (Israel), Simon (Peter), and Saul (Paul). The fact that Levi is referred to elsewhere as Matthew may reveal that leaving the tax collection station was his life-changing event. Some scholars believe that once a Jew stopped being a tax collector, he could never return to the profession.

The Latin term *publican* refers to a class of people holding a state contract to collect taxes or perform other civil service functions.

The word *sinners* probably refers to common people who did not practice the strict rituals of the Pharisees.

Christ's story about the wedding feast was probably a subtle reminder to John the Baptist's disciples that Christ was indeed the groom. See John 3:26-36.

The storage of liquids was a continual problem in Palestine. Wine was often stored in new goatskins that had been stitched together to form an irregularly shaped vessel. Once the skins dried out, they could no longer be used to store new wine that produced gas during the fermentation process. Christ used a common practice to teach a powerful truth.

illustrated lesson about His power over sin and about His deity when He restored the man's health. The physical healing pointed to the reality of the spiritual healing. The scribes could do neither.

Christ's next actions struck right at the heart of the most outwardly pious members of Jewish society. He called Levi, or Matthew, a tax collector, to be one of His disciples. He then attended a dinner with Levi's associates who were characterized by the Pharisees as "publicans and sinners." Tax collectors worked for King Herod and for the Romans. They had great power to search and to take property for the treasury and for themselves. Most Jews hated these people for their cruelty and for their association with the foreign government. The Pharisees rigorously separated themselves from such notable sinners.

Jesus took a much different approach to the situation. Levi probably sat near the boat docks at Capernaum to collect taxes on both imports and exports. He heard Jesus preaching around the shore and responded to Jesus' invitation. Levi's dinner gave Jesus an opportunity to preach to a group of people often excluded from the synagogue and from mainstream Jewish society. Christ explained to the Pharisees that the tax collectors were sick and needed a doctor, which was a common proverb about compassion at the time. Notice that Jesus implied that He was the doctor. Also, He told them plainly that His mission was to call "sinners to repentance." The Pharisees' desire for outward piety through total separation from sinners failed to meet God's desire to reach those sinful men.

The next scene (Mark 2:18-22) involves Christ, the disciples of John the Baptist, and the Pharisees in a conversation about fasting. Moses' law required fasting on the great Day of Atonement, which occurred one day each year. Through the years, the Jews began to fast more often as a means to draw closer to God. The Pharisees fasted twice per week according to Luke 18:12.

It is important to note that Jesus did not condemn the practice, but encouraged fasting privately and not as a public demonstration. Jesus used a familiar wedding custom to tell them that His disciples would fast at a later date. For now, they would not fast

82

## Demonstration: New and Old Cloth

**Goal:** To demonstrate Christ's teaching about new things.

**Procedure:** Cut a hole in an old shirt and sew a piece of new cotton fabric over the hole. Show the students the shirt and then wash it in hot water. Show the students again. Ask the students to state the lesson of the shirt. Emphasize the newness and superior

nature of a relationship with Christ over dead religion.

because He was still with them. He also used two parable-like comparisons to announce that He was setting aside traditional practices in favor of something new. The man-made constraints of their religion could not hold the forthcoming power and victory of a relationship with God through Christ.

Strict Sabbath observances also characterized the Pharisees' religion. Mark tells us that the Pharisees watched Jesus and the disciples walking through a grain field. The disciples picked some of the grain, removed the chaff, and then ate. The Pharisees accused Jesus of not controlling His disciples by exclaiming, "Behold, why do they on the Sabbath day that which is not lawful" (Mark 2:23-28). Old Testament law did prohibit work on the Sabbath in order to give people physical rest and the time for worship. It allowed acts of kindness and compassion to meet human needs. Jesus also argued in Luke 14:5 that men rescued their animals that had fallen into pits on the Sabbath out of a sense of compassion.

The Sabbath day was God's gift to man and was not to be a tool for oppression. The "law" referred to by the Pharisees was their own oral tradition created by rabbis through the years. They identified thirty-nine types of work and many more subtypes that were prohibited on the Sabbath. Simple tasks were often equated with work. Pulling out a hair was the equivalent of shearing sheep. Picking a few heads of grain corresponded to reaping a field. Jesus reminded them of a time when King David ate some bread that was only for the priests. His actions broke the letter of the law, but upheld the spirit of the law, which is compassion for the needs of men. Jesus also reminded the Pharisees that the Sabbath was created for man's benefit, and that He controlled the specific manner of Sabbath observances. Again, Jesus asserted His deity and authority while laying aside the man-made religion of the Pharisees.

See Exodus 20:10 for the prohibition of work on the Sabbath.

See Deuteronomy 23:25 for regulations about eating a small amount of grain from a neighbor's field. The practice would aid those traveling far from home and their normal food supply. Notice also that the rights of the owner are protected by the prohibition against using a sickle to gather large amounts of grain.

See I Samuel 21 for the account of David's eating the sacred bread.

The Pharisees prohibited healing on the Sabbath because of
the elaborate ceremonies used
in the process. Christ used
none of the ceremonies and
they still condemned Him. The
Pharisees then failed to understand the basis of their own
tradition as it applied to the
situation before them.

Mark 3:34; 5:32; 10:23; and
11:11 record Christ's looking at
various things.

Mark now turns our attention to a synagogue service in Capernaum (Mark 3:1-6). The Pharisees watched Christ to entangle Him
in a violation of their teachings. Healing was strictly prohibited on
the Sabbath according to their tradition. A man with a withered, or
useless, hand was present. An ancient historical reference indicates
that he was a stonemason or a plasterer. If the reference is accurate,
the man was in a desperate condition because he could not work in
his profession. Jesus gave the Pharisees an opportunity to acknowledge the true meaning of the Sabbath. When they refused to answer, Jesus healed the man by simply speaking to him. They heard
the teaching of Christ and witnessed His power and compassion.
Instead of rejoicing with the healed man and trying to learn more
of Christ, they conspired with the Herodians to kill Him. Edmond
Hiebert correctly observes that the Pharisees "regarded it a terrible
crime for Jesus to heal on the Sabbath, but they had no qualms
about plotting murder on the Sabbath!" (Hiebert, 87).

## Conspiracy Against Christ
### Mark 3:7–14:42

The curiosity of the local religious leaders now extended to
the religious establishment in Jerusalem. In the last chapter, we
studied the evil accusation of the Jerusalem scribes as recorded in
Mark 3:22-30. Christ continued His ministry in spite of the criti-
cism. In fact, more people seemed to follow Christ after that incident. The hostility of the scribes and Pharisees also increased.
They looked for ways to trap and to condemn Jesus.

We will not have time to examine each confrontation between
Jesus and the religious leaders. You may study them on your own
or as a class exercise. We will watch as Christ defends Himself
against foolish accusations and challenges the entrenched practices of the day. Jesus wanted to clearly distinguish Himself from
the traditions and to warn everyone, including the scribes and
Pharisees, about the danger of clinging to a defective religion. In
every case, the defect centered on a failure either to know or to
apply the Word of God properly. Once again, each scene shows us
the glory of knowing Christ personally.

84

## Overhead: Christ Versus Religion

**Goal:** To contrast failed and true religion.

**Procedure:** See the Christ Versus
Religion overheads in the Appendix
(pp. 155-56). One is blank for use in
the discussion. The other has been
filled out with suggested verses and
applications. Ask the students to list
pairs of things that contrast with each
other. Examples include light and
darkness, sweet and sour, and black
and white. During lecture and discussion about Christ's conflicts with the
religious establishment, fill out the
chart. Toward the end of the chapter,
review the data and begin to make applications to the situation in your community and to the students. Make
sharp contrasts between religion and
Christ.

In Mark 7, another group of scribes and Pharisees came from Jerusalem to watch Jesus and to try to discredit His ministry. They saw some of the disciples eating a meal without going through the elaborate hand-washing ceremonies. Mark devotes two verses to explaining the custom for the benefit of non-Jewish readers. About thirty chapters of the Talmud discuss all the procedures and practices for washing both hands and pots. The process of purification was one of the central themes of the Pharisees' religion. According to their own words, the ritual came from the "tradition of the elders" and not from the law of Moses (Mark 7:5). The word *tradition* occurs five times in this chapter. We can therefore conclude that Jesus' words constitute His formal evaluation of the Jewish customs.

John 2:1-11, the account of the wedding feast at Cana of Galilee, provides a glimpse into the custom of purification and washing. The location of the feast was probably the home of a Pharisee.

See Isaiah 29:13.

*Corban* is an Aramaic word that means "gift."

Notice that He first turned their attention to the prophet Isaiah. God used Isaiah to condemn outward religion that never reaches the heart. The source of this defective religion is the replacement of God's Word with man's traditions. Jesus then recounted to them their practice of dishonoring parents. The Pharisees would vow to give all their money to the temple. If elderly parents needed financial assistance, the Pharisee would refuse to give it to them based on the fact that it was devoted to God. The result was an impoverished parent and the breaking of the fifth commandment (Exod. 20:12). Tradition supplanted God's very clear precept of honoring parents.

Jesus then called the multitude together and exposed the theological fallacy practiced by the religious leadership. Traditional Jewish theology taught that man is good, and that he may choose good or evil based on external influences. Conforming to outward standards of conduct pointed to inward purity. Jesus told the multitude—and later the disciples—that man is only defiled by what

Judaism has been called the religion of ethical monotheism. The system denies original sin and the resulting human depravity. Man is inwardly good, but can be influenced to evil by external forces.

Traditional Christianity teaches that Adam's sin corrupted the entire race and that man is inwardly evil. Only the supernatural work of God through Christ can cleanse man's sin. Much of Paul's Epistle to the Romans delineates the specifics of this doctrine.

85

---

### Discussion: Pious Disobedience

**Goal:** To emphasize that all disobedience is sin.

**Procedure:** Divide the class into several small groups and assign each group one or two of the Ten Commandments. Instruct each group to create a one-minute skit based on how modern people break the commandments and then justify their actions. Each group then presents its

skit, and the rest of the class identifies the broken commandment. For better class control, consider having the students write out the skits and turn them in for review. Choose the best one or two for presentation.

### Discussion: Robes of Piety

**Goal:** To expose self-righteousness in modern religion.

**Procedure:** Ask each of the students to write on the board one rule that

your school enforces. Review the reasons for the various rules. Ask the students if keeping all the rules makes them acceptable to God. Point out the difference between keeping the rules to impress men or God and keeping the rules out of love for God. Encourage the students to examine themselves for self-righteousness. Emphasize that Christ is our righteousness.

See the Appendix (p. 165) for a list of recommended commentaries. Liberal commentators often embroil themselves in speculative debates about the origin and genuineness of the text. Most reject plenary verbal inspiration. Before using a commentary, read the preface and the introduction to discern the author's theological position. Avoid those that hold to a weak view of inspiration.

## Commentaries: Tools for Understanding

Bible scholars often write books to help Christians understand the text and application of the Scriptures. When studying the Bible, you should always read the text several times and record your thoughts on paper. Use a dictionary to look up unfamiliar words. Try to find the main teaching of the passage. Then, use a conservative commentary to supply details about the culture, language, and interpretation of the verses.

One very good commentary on Mark is Edmond Hiebert's *The Gospel of Mark*, published by BJU Press. The following selection deals with Jesus' warning to the disciples about the teachings of the Pharisees in Mark 8:15.

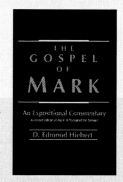

"Take heed . . . beware of"—the utterance of a double caution. Both verbs are present imperatives, stressing attitudes that ought to continue. The first verb calls for mental alertness, while the second demands that they look attentively at the object called to their attention in order to avoid the danger it presents.

"The leaven of the Pharisees and of the leaven of Herod"—the repeated definite noun, *the leaven*, views the two leavens as distinct yet closely related as a common moral danger because both were allied against Christ. Since leaven was strictly forbidden with certain offerings (Lev. 2:11) and had to be removed during the Passover, it readily became a figure of evil or corruption. This was the meaning given it in rabbinical teaching and seems to be its uniform meaning in the New Testament. As producing a process of fermentation, leaven or yeast pictures a pervasive corrupting tendency that works invisibly. Christ's warning was thus "a pithy one-word parable for unseen pervasive influence." Mark did not give us an interpretation of Christ's meaning, but Matthew (16:12) noted that His reference was to "the teaching" of those warned against. Clearly Christ was thinking of the penetrating and corrupting influence of the teachings of His opponents. His warning against the leaven of the Pharisees is to be understood in the light of what had just occurred [Mark 8:11-13]. Their perverted views concerning moral goodness and moral evil (cf. 7:1-23) left them morally blind and unable to discern the mission and character of the Messiah (Hiebert, 226).

86

### Exercise: Student Teachers

**Goal:** To gain truth from personal study of the Scripture.

**Procedure:** Instruct each student to develop a short devotional teaching session from Mark 8:14-21. The student should read the passage five times, write one sentence about the main teaching or theme, explain why the particular theme was chosen by explaining the passage, and then apply the theme to modern life. Use the selection in the text from Hiebert for help. Grade the work and allow one or two students to present their thoughts to the class.

comes out of him. External influences do not defile. The sinful operation of man's heart defiles. Man's problem is not failing to wash hands and pots. It is internal wickedness that only Christ cures through the forgiveness of sins and the beginning of an entirely new life. Many people probably did not understand the magnitude of Christ's words. New life comes not from external ritual, but from embracing the Son of God.

Christ entered the temple near the time of the crucifixion and removed those who used the temple grounds as a marketplace (Mark 11:15-18). The high priest did not allow the use of foreign coins bearing the image of Caesar for the purchase of items needed in worship. Jews from all over the world arrived in Jerusalem to sacrifice and to worship. These travelers required animals and provisions. The priest's family gladly exchanged their Roman coins for temple coins and then sold sacrificial animals at inflated prices. Jesus saw those in the religious establishment using their positions to make money and to exploit faithful Jews. His righteous actions infuriated the scribes and priests.

When Jesus returned to the temple a short time after His expulsion of the money exchangers and merchants, the religious leaders asked Him about the source of His authority. Jesus turned the question back to their rejection of John the Baptist's preaching. Mark 12 then records the final public debate between Christ and the religious leaders. Jesus began by telling the people

The streets leading to the temple contained numerous shops selling items needed in worship. Around the time of Christ, the priests allowed the merchants to enter the outer courts of the temple complex.

87

## Exercise: Choral Reading

**Goal:** To remember the words of Scripture.

**Procedure:** Divide the class into groups of three of four students. Assign one section of Mark 12 to each group. Instruct the students to choose one person to be Christ, another to be a religious leader, and others to be narrators. Allow sufficient time for the students to practice the characterization of their parts. Encourage the use of appropriate props. Have each group then present their selection to the class. You may want to ask for some help from the school speech department.

gathered at the temple a parable about wicked tenant farmers rejecting the owner's messengers and his expectations for fruit. The language reflects a similar story in Isaiah 5 that would have been familiar to the learned scribes. Notice that Jesus implied that He was the son of the owner, a reference to His deity. He also quoted from Psalm 118:22, 23 to tell them that God Himself will overrule the scribes and Pharisees' rejection of the Messiah. The very people that should have been the first to recognize and embrace the Messiah seemed utterly blinded by their religion and greed.

The Pharisees, Herodians, Sadducees, and scribes seem to present Jesus with their most vexing questions. Rabbinical literature contains many debates that are often not understood by western cultures. The temple confrontations clearly show the superiority of Christ over the major sects of the day.

Next, the leaders sent a delegation of Pharisees and Herodians to Jesus to entrap Him in one of the most difficult questions of the time for the Jews. The Roman government imposed heavy taxes on all conquered provinces. The Jews believed that paying the tax was equivalent to accepting Caesar's rule over the sacred land. Failure to pay might provoke military action by the Roman legion. Perhaps they believed that the Romans might take Jesus away if He advocated not paying. If He agreed to pay the tax, then the Pharisees would accuse Him of collusion with the enemy. Jesus looked at a coin and said, "Render to Caesar the things that are Caesar's, and to God the things that are God's" (Mark 12:17). Duties to God and duties to government do not conflict in the issue of tax payments.

The Sadducees then asked Jesus a theoretical question about eternity and the resurrection from the dead (Mark 12:18-27). This group did not believe in the resurrection, and therefore asked the question to entangle Jesus in heresy in order to condemn Him. It's possible that the Sadducees used the same story to frustrate the Pharisees.

Jesus directly rebuked them for being ignorant of the Old Testament Scriptures. He pointed out that heaven is not like earth. Marriage does not exist in eternity; therefore the question is not

See a Bible encyclopedia or the Internet for more information about Herod's temple.

### Herod's Temple

**HISTORICAL LIGHT**

Jerusalem was the center of national pride and worship for Jews around the world. Herod the Great decided that building a magnificent temple in the city would ensure the loyalty of his divided subjects and would establish his kingdom. The project began in 20 B.C. and was not completed until A.D. 64. Priests, trained by Herod, performed most of the work. Josephus wrote that the white marble and gold structures glistened in the sun and could be seen for miles. As the hub of Jewish religion, the temple contained the furniture, rooms, and equipment for the ritual sacrifices. The New Testament contains many references to Herod's temple. It was destroyed by the Romans in A.D. 70—only six years after its completion.

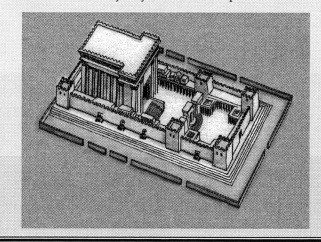

relevant. Jesus also gave them a lesson in explaining the books of Moses that they claimed to believe. God's statement to Moses at the burning bush implies that Abraham, Isaac, and Jacob lived at that very moment. The book of Genesis records the death of all three. The only reasonable conclusion is that God had raised them from the dead. Every detail of this doctrine may not be clear, but the Sadducees had no excuse for missing the point of the Scriptures.

Finally, a scribe came to Jesus and presented Him with another vexing question (Mark 12:28-34). Jews often debated which commandment was the greatest. Jesus' answer combined two positive

89

The Scriptures record Christ's contact with several leaders of the religious establishment that were honestly seeking for God. These men included Nicodemus (John 3), Jairus (Mark 5), Joseph of Arimathaea (Mark 15), and the unnamed scribe (Mark 12).

aspects of Old Testament religion. The first comes from Deuteronomy 6:4, 5, which states the uniqueness of God's person and man's duty to love Him. He then quoted a more obscure passage from Leviticus 19:18 that summarizes the duties of one man to other men. Note that love is the primary requirement in both situations. The scribe commended Jesus for His wise answer and affirmed that loving God supersedes all sacrifice and ritual. Not every religious leader in Israel was blind to the true intent of the Scriptures.

Jesus had started this debate by asking the religious leaders about John the Baptist's ministry. He ended it by asking about the proper interpretation of Psalm 110, which was universally accepted by the Jews as pointing to the Messiah (Mark 12:35-40). The scribes preached that Messiah would be a direct descendant of King David. In earthly relationships, fathers exercise authority over children. The scribes therefore believed that Messiah would submit to David as a son submitted to a father. Jesus quoted Psalm 110:1, in which David calls Messiah by the title "my Lord."

In Jewish thought, a father would never call a child "my Lord." The leaders failed to understand that Messiah was more than a physical descendant of David. Messiah was both God and man through the miracle of the incarnation. Jesus wanted to show them the weakness of their interpretations and teachings. The common man in the temple probably rejoiced that Jesus had confounded the scribes and Pharisees. Jesus then sternly warned the people to beware of the blatant hypocrisy of the religious leadership. In contrast, He noted the simple godliness of a poor widow contributing to the temple treasury (Mark 12:41-44).

## Temple Activities

**Goal:** To recognize the temple as the center of Jewish religious life.

**Procedure:** Divide the class into groups of three or four students. Ask the students to find and write down the references and a very brief description of examples of temple activity in the Gospels. Set a time limit of fifteen minutes. Allow each group to announce their findings one at a time. If another group has the same reference, all groups should eliminate that reference from their lists. When all groups finish their lists, the winner is the group that has the most references remaining. Encourage the use of reference Bibles or concordances for this exercise.

## Condemnation of Christ
### Mark 14:43–15:47

Jesus knew exactly what the religious establishment planned to do with Him. He also knew that God had planned His death to bring about man's eternal salvation from sin. His task was to obey God and to deliver one last direct witness of the truth to the leaders of Israel. The critical moment came as the leaders brought Jesus to trial before the Sanhedrin in Mark 14:53-65. Jesus did not respond as witnesses presented conflicting evidence of His guilt. Finally, out of a sense of frustration, the high priest asked Jesus directly, "Art thou the Christ, the Son of the Blessed?" The question probably echoed what the high priest had heard about Jesus and does not indicate that the man believed it. Again, he was looking for a way to trap Jesus and to give them an excuse to kill Him. This time, Jesus answered in such a way as to prick their consciences with the truth that they claimed to believe. "I am" could be a direct reference to the Old Testament name of God given to Moses at the burning bush (Exod. 3:14).

The Jews reverenced this name to the point that they would not speak it for fear of defiling God's character in some way. Jesus' response could also be a shortened form of "I am the Christ, the Son of the Blessed." Either way, the message was clear. Jesus confessed His true identity. He likewise alluded to His coming judgment upon their sin by using language similar to that in Daniel 7:13 and Psalm 110:1. Christ's confession should have caused them to stop and consider this person whom they wanted to condemn. But they rushed forward with a sentence of guilt and took Jesus to Pilate for the official death sentence. The Romans did not empower the Jewish council to put anyone to death.

The high priest, acting as the chief political and religious figure in Israel, convened a meeting with the other religious leaders to plan a believable indictment of Christ before the Roman governor (Mark 15:1). Pilate finally accepted the guilty verdict and crucified Jesus. In one last act of cruelty and rejection, the leaders mocked Christ as He hung on the cross (Mark 15:31, 32).

Matthew Henry points out that the workers of wickedness are very diligent in the performance of their business. Also notice how the differing factions work together to condemn Christ. Historical documents show that these groups frequently disagreed vehemently on almost every issue.

Man may never fully comprehend the wonders of God's work at Christ's trial and Crucifixion. God planned the event in ages past and used the prophets to announce it to His people (Isaiah 53 and others). God then allowed wicked men to carry out their own desires, resulting in the fulfillment of His plan. Christ, in humility and in subjection to the Father's will, died in shame at the cruel hand of a Roman governor.

To be effective in the classroom and in life, we must do more than teach the facts of Christ's death. We must allow God's enormous love for us to overwhelm our hearts. In the darkness of man's religion, we can better see the contrasting greatness of God's compassion. It will be much easier for the students to shun false religion when they see the fruits of true righteousness in us.

91

## Accusations Against Christ

**Goal:** Consider the wicked actions of the religious and political leaders at Christ's trial.

**Procedure:** Discuss the facts of the trial and Crucifixion of Christ from Mark 14 and 15. Ask the following questions and encourage a discussion of each.

Q: What were the two indictments against Christ?

A: Religious leaders—Christ claimed to be the Messiah and God's Son.

A: Pilate—Christ was the king of the Jews.

Q: Were the indictments true?

A: Yes

Q: What was the real issue?

A: The people did not believe the truth.

Q: Do you believe the truth?

Three days later, the disciples wondered and rejoiced over the fulfillment of Psalm 118:22, 23: "The stone which the builders refused is become the head stone of the corner. This is the Lord's doing; it is marvellous in our eyes." Christ rose from the dead to vindicate His authority and teaching. Even so, the Gospel of Matthew records the scheme of the religious leaders to discredit the Resurrection (Matt. 28:11-15).

The Mocking of Christ, *by Northern follower of Caravaggio, Bob Jones University Collection*

## Final Thoughts

The Bible portrays the best and worst of man's nature: the depravity of the wicked religious leaders helps us to better discern the glory of Jesus Christ. Even the very best of men will disappoint you at some time. As you survey religious movements and organizations today, you are very likely to see many characteristics of the scribes and Pharisees. Let those perceptions drive you to a close relationship with the Son of God. Rejecting man's religious traditions in favor of God's clear teaching in the Bible will bring the scorn of many people. The Lord may be opening an opportunity for you to present the truth to them. They rejected Christ and they may reject you. If following Christ means walking contrary to man's religion, then so be it. "That I may know him" must be the goal of our lives.

92

## Discussion: Religion Today

**Goal:** To apply the teaching of Christ to modern religion.

**Procedure:** Gather information on specific religious movements, functions, activities, and doctrinal statements. The Internet or local newspaper will provide many examples. Compare the information about modern religious groups to the characteristics of the scribes and Pharisees in Mark. Note specifically their attitude toward God's Word, the person and work of Christ, and the means of righteousness. Apply the same procedure to the lives of the students. Emphasize that religion is useless and that a relationship with Christ is the key to true life. Invite those who have questions or doubts to speak to you privately after class.

# Review Questions

## Matching

A. Traditions
B. Not in NT
C. 70
D. Priests
E. Disciple

F. Pilate
G. Tax collector
H. Followers of a king
I. Temple builder
J. Law experts

_J_ 1.  Scribes

_A_ 2.  Pharisees

_H_ 3.  Herodians

_B_ 4.  Essenes

_C_ 5.  Sanhedrin

_F_ 6. Governor

_I_ 7. Herod the Great

_G_ 8. Publican

_D_ 9. Sadducees

## Essay

10. Why did the scribes and Pharisees consider Jesus to be a threat?

   *Jesus exposed the shallowness of their religion.*

11. Why were the Pharisees upset that Jesus associated with the publicans?

   *Most Jews hated the publicans' association with foreign control and taxation. The Pharisees separated themselves from sinful elements in society and expected Jesus to do the same.*

12. What is the "tradition of the elders"?

*The tradition of the elders is a body of oral teachings passed down through the generations of rabbis. The Pharisees held to the traditions. Jesus rejected the traditions as the teachings of man.*

13. Why did the priest prohibit Roman coins in the temple?

*The Roman coins represented Roman control, which was not acceptable to the priests. The image of Caesar appeared on the coins, and the Jews believed the image was idolatrous. The prohibition also gave the priest the opportunity to make a significant profit by exchanging Roman coins for temple coins.*

14. How did Jesus summarize the law of Moses in Mark 12?

*Jesus told a scribe that the highest teaching of the law was first, love for God, and second, love for man.*

15. Why did the Jewish leaders condemn Christ at His trial?

*The leaders condemned Christ because He exposed their wickedness and because He confessed His identity as the Son of God. The leaders did not believe the works or the words of Christ. They were blinded by their religion.*

CHAPTER SIX

# Christel and the Disciples—Part I

6

Beth Kent flipped through the pages of her music scrapbook. Beth's mother took pictures at every recital and concert, and also collected the programs and awards. She then assembled the articles onto the pages of a large scrapbook. At first, Beth had thought that her mother's efforts were a waste of time. But now that she was nearly ready to graduate from high school, she enjoyed looking at the pages before a concert. Remembering the years of hard work seemed to help her get ready to play her instrument. Beth was now the principal cellist in the high school orchestra. Mr. Fredrick, the orchestra conductor, depended on her leadership to help the younger musicians play together and stay in tune.

Beth's mother came into the room and sat down beside her. They turned to the beginning of the book where Beth was shown in second grade, just starting to play piano. The tiny quarter-size cello first appeared in fourth grade, the year she started taking lessons. By seventh grade, she had a half-size cello and braces on her teeth. The braces disappeared in tenth grade. By then she also had a full-size cello and several awards for playing excellence.

"What do you notice about every page in the scrapbook from fourth grade until now?" her mom asked.

Beth quickly turned through a dozen or more pages and the answer seemed obvious.

### Goals

Students should

1. Recognize the deity of Christ.
2. Understand the process of discipleship.
3. Desire closer fellowship with Christ.
4. Evaluate their personal relationships to Christ.

### Objectives

Students should be able to

1. State evidences of Christ's deity.
2. Explain basic decisions required for discipleship.
3. Discuss the purposes for events in the Gospels.
4. Use standard tools and methods for effective Bible study.
5. Analyze facts in the accounts to formulate conclusions.

### Scripture Reading

1. Mark 1-8
2. John 1-6

### Memory Verses

1. Mark 1:17
2. Mark 4:39, 40
3. Mark 8:34, 35

95

## Lecture Overview

### Introduction

1. Success is partly the result of hard work over time.
2. Discipleship requires diligently following Christ over time.

### The Call to Discipleship

1. Disciples are followers of a teacher.
2. Christ seeks men to follow Him.

3. Christ's disciples were ordinary men.

### Calming the Sea

1. Christ controls nature.
2. Christ teaches men about His deity.

### Ministering in the Villages

1. Jesus teaches by having the disciples work by themselves.
2. Jesus places great importance on the disciples' work.

## Cooperating in the Ministry I

1. Christ's methods and plans surpass human reasoning.
2. Christ acts in an orderly manner.
3. Christ uses the disciples to meet a need.

**95**

**Thoughts for the Teacher**

1. Remember that reading the text of Mark will significantly affect the students. See the Appendix (p. 134) for ideas.

2. God will bless a teacher's fervent prayer for the success of the Word with the students.

3. Modern Christians view discipleship as a set of activities. Stress that the real issue is a vital relationship to Christ.

4. Some students will experience difficulties in submitting to Christ's teaching and authority. The orderliness of your classroom procedures and expectations will aid struggling students.

5. The disciples failed many times and so will the students. Be persistent in presenting the truth. Do not give up on students who do not seem interested. Only God knows the heart. The Lord can use your teaching to penetrate the hardest heart.

"Mom, Mrs. Matthews is everywhere! She is either teaching me, sitting in the front row of the audience during a concert, or standing next to me during an award presentation."

Mrs. Kent said, "Do you remember when she informed us that you had little chance for success with the cello? You started practicing for forty-five minutes every day just to prove her wrong!"

"I well remember that day. I think she was just trying to get me going! After nine years of weekly lessons with her, the thing that I appreciate the most is that Mrs. Matthews can play cello better than anyone else I know. She explains techniques and music theory, but then she shows me how to do it. Playing with her is the very best part of learning cello."

Her mother interrupted her and said, "Your dad and I appreciate Mrs. Matthews's determination to make you a good cello player. But, if we don't leave soon, you will be late for the concert, and all of us will be in trouble!"

The Kents arrived in plenty of time for the performance. Parents, classmates, teachers, and friends enjoyed every minute of the hour-long concert. And of course, Mrs. Matthews sat right in the front row.

96

## Teachings on the Sea

1. Jesus repeats lessons due to our failure to learn the first time.

2. Jesus designs and uses adversity to teach the disciples about Himself.

3. Disciples must focus on the person of Christ.

## Cooperating in the Ministry II

1. Christ designed the circumstances to teach important lessons about Himself.

2. Christ expected the disciples to learn.

## Training for Discipleship

1. Jesus revealed the true nature and mission of the Messiah.

2. Jesus revealed the true nature and actions of discipleship.

## Some Final Thoughts

1. Review

2. Discipleship still means following Christ.

## Supplemental Resource: *Basics for Believers*

*Basics for Believers* by James A. Berg is an excellent short workbook on Christian growth. The question-and-answer format teaches basic discipleship from the New Testament. The book could be used as a supplemental text, as homework, or as a guide for having the students teach the class. See bjup.com for ordering information.

Once, after hearing a talented musician, I tried to teach myself how to play the piano. After a few hours, I could tap out one or two lines of a song, but I soon gave up. Piano was a lot of work and required more dedication than I was willing to put into it by myself. Perhaps a teacher could have guided me about timing and hand techniques. Being responsible to a teacher could have motivated me to keep trying and to make steady progress. Beth's skill at the cello was due in part to her relationship with her teacher.

Many young Christians approach their relationship to Christ as I approached the piano. We want the benefits, but are unwilling to learn from the Teacher. Being a disciple of Christ does place some demands upon us. Jesus constantly teaches us lessons, and we must respond accordingly. In this chapter, we will examine Christ's program for developing His followers. By carefully learning from our master teacher and then following His example, my life as a believer will grow and flourish. I may never be able to play the piano or the cello due to my lack of talent and skill. But I can follow Christ. More importantly, He can transform my life into something truly productive for the kingdom of God.

## The Call to Discipleship
### Mark 1:16-20; 3:13-19

The Gospel of John records Jesus' first personal contact with some of the disciples (John 1:35-51). John the Baptist openly identified Jesus as the Lamb of God and then encouraged his disciples to follow Jesus. These men recognized Jesus as a Rabbi or teacher (John 1:38), as the Messiah (John 1:41), and as the Son of God and King of Israel (John 1:49). We may assume that Christ's public teachings and private conversations helped them to understand His person. The text does not indicate that they stayed with Him all the time. As Jesus preached around Galilee and Jordan, they gladly listened and believed.

Mark's first mention of the disciples, in Mark 1:16-20, actually occurred in the second year of Jesus' public ministry. Nearly a year later—after Herod had imprisoned John the Baptist—Jesus once again ministered in Galilee. This is when He called two sets

Jesus wisely designed the one-year delay between the initial belief and the call into full-time discipleship. The time allowed the men to observe and hear Christ more fully and to evaluate the poverty of their earthly occupations. Spiritual growth is often a slow process.

Notice the three types of fishing in this account. The men caught fish. Christ caught the men. Christ wanted to teach the men how to catch other men.

James and John appear to have left wealth and a prosperous fishing business to follow Christ. The Greek word translated "ship" indicates a large vessel. Most fishing boats were relatively small. Also, only successful businesses could afford hired servants.

---

## Discussion: Moving Toward Excellence

**Goal:** To encourage realistic thinking about improvement.

**Procedure:** Ask the students to list five well-known people who are outstanding in their field. Challenge them to determine how these people obtained excellence. Point out that the majority have had one or more teachers or coaches and that they have spent much time working at their particular

skills. Conclude by encouraging them to understand that spiritual growth requires a teacher, effort, and time.

## Exercise: Motivators

**Goal:** To expose basic motivations for discipleship.

**Procedure:** Bring to class several items that represent typical motivators for teens. Examples may include food, trophies, money, and pillows. Ask the class to tell you why these items moti-

vate people. Instruct the students to write down what motivated the disciples to follow Christ and what motivates the students to follow Christ. Allow them to share answers with the class.

of brothers to follow Him full-time. Notice that Jesus used language that the fishermen would readily understand. Their fathers had taught them the fishing business; now Jesus wanted to teach them how to fish for men. *Come ye after me* simply means to follow. Teachers in ancient times would walk from one place to the next while students walked behind or beside them. Students would listen and ask questions along the way. Simon, Andrew, James, and John quickly left their fishing business to learn the much greater business of reaching men.

Some months later, the Jewish religious leadership began to oppose Christ's ministry and teaching. By that time, large crowds followed Jesus because they recognized His great power and authority. Jesus personally selected twelve men for two important purposes. Mark 3:14 says that these men "should be with him," which indicates a special closeness to and fellowship with the Teacher. The same verse also tells us that He would "send them forth to preach." We get the English word *apostle* from the Greek word translated "send forth." These were Jesus' disciples and apostles. He would first teach them about God's kingdom, and then send them out to preach the gospel.

Let's briefly examine some facts about these twelve men. All, except for perhaps Judas Iscariot, were from Galilee and not from the center of Jewish religion in Jerusalem. None were scribes, priests, or Pharisees. Matthew worked for the government as a tax collector. Simon the Canaanite or Zealot opposed the government through sabotage and subversion. James and John, nicknamed by Jesus as the sons of thunder, were probably emotional and restless. Logically, we might expect Jesus to choose high-class religious leaders as His closest associates for spreading God's Word to Israel. Instead, He selected lowly men who responded to His Word. They left jobs, businesses, families, and other personal interests to follow the Son of God and to seek the souls of men.

Many of the disciples' names listed in Mark 3 have Aramaic origins. Scholars believe that Jesus often used the Aramaic language in His preaching and with the disciples.

## Calming the Sea
### Mark 4:35-41

Christ's training of the disciples now took a new direction. They had just completed a day of public instruction and private lessons about the kingdom of God. Jesus was tired and so were the disciples. To escape the multitudes and to get some rest, He directed them to take a boat to the other side of the lake. As the fishermen sailed across the water, Jesus slept on a pillow in the back of the ship. Suddenly a great storm of wind and waves came upon them.

The Sea of Galilee is actually over six hundred feet below sea level and is surrounded by many mountains. The warm waters attract violent weather even today. High winds kicked up waves that filled the boat with water. Some of the disciples probably bailed water out of the boat. Others tried to steady the sail or held on to the side to keep from being thrown overboard. "Carest thou not that we perish?" shows us that the fishermen's skill and experience on the water was no match for the storm. The words seem to rebuke Jesus for sleeping and for showing little concern for their dire condition.

Jesus was now ready to teach them an important lesson about Himself. As the Son of God, the waves were not a threat to Him. He simply got up from the pillow and calmed the storm by His word. The howling wind stopped immediately when Jesus commanded *Peace,* which means "be quiet" or "be silent." *Be still* comes from a word that means "to be muzzled." Jesus then rebuked the disciples for their lack of faith, which had turned to

Observe the attributes of Christ in this account.

Humanity: He slept due to tiredness.

Deity: He calmed the sea and knew that the sea was not a threat to the group.

Compassion: He calmed the sea to remove the disciples' fears. He rebuked the disciples for lack of faith, which was the primary issue.

99

## Exercise: The Geography of Galilee

**Goal:** To familiarize the students with Bible geography.

**Procedure:** Use books on Bible geography, reference Bibles, encyclopedias, and the Internet to gather information about the Sea of Galilee and surrounding areas. Assign a written report, a few simple drawings, or a group report as the means of conveying the research data to the class.

fearfulness. He fully expected them to recognize His deity. Had He not cast out demons and healed many of the sick? The disciples now feared Jesus more than they feared the storm. A true disciple of Christ will recognize that Jesus is God and will rest in His concern for him.

## Ministering in the Villages
### Mark 6:7-13

The people of Nazareth did not accept the teachings of Christ. He understood that opposition to His work would increase as time passed. He also knew that the disciples needed to learn some important lessons about the nature of the ministry. Sending the disciples to the villages would certainly spread the news of salvation to more people, and it would also give the twelve some very valuable experiences. They listened to Jesus' teaching, saw His great compassion, and experienced His power over the sea. Now they must learn by doing the work that Jesus did. But this time, the disciples would do it without Jesus' presence.

Notice that he sent them out in teams of two. Old Testament law required two witnesses to an event. A single person could make up a wild story or bring a false accusation against another. The Israelites were to dismiss the claims of a single source. Jesus

wanted the disciples to have credibility, and so He wisely sent them two by two. Likewise, Jesus gave them authority over unclean spirits so that people would listen more attentively to their preaching.

He gave them very strict instructions about physical provisions along the way. They could take the shoes, clothing, and the walking stick of a common poor traveler, and nothing else. Jesus wanted to teach them to depend upon God for their daily provisions. He also wanted them to avoid

100

See the following verses regarding working in pairs: Deuteronomy 19:15; Ecclesiastes 4:9-12; Luke 7:19; Acts 13:2, 3; 15:39-41; 19:22.

The Bible contains nearly fifty direct references to Sodom and Gomorrah. See Genesis 19 for the account of God's judgment on these cities.

Customary hospitality for Jewish travelers included lodging and food.

Modern educators recognize the value of learning by doing. The best teachers use a variety of instructional methods, as did Jesus.

## Exercise: Ministering for Christ

**Goal:** To learn by doing.

**Procedure:** Design a ministry project for the class. Examples include tract distribution, teaching a Bible class to a lower grade, organizing a chapel program, or any other project that requires effort in ministry. At the conclusion of the project, ask the class to share what they learned about themselves, other

people, and the Lord. Encourage further involvement.

## Exercise: Ask a Missionary

**Goal:** To understand that the Lord teaches us as we work for Him.

**Procedure:** Ask a missionary to come to class and talk about God's provision for his work, the type of work engaged in, results, and lessons learned. Allow the students to ask questions.

If a missionary is not available, gather enough prayer letters for each student to have one. Have the student read the letter and look for the information listed above.

100

### The Fish Symbol

Early Christians used the fish as a symbol of their faith. When meeting a stranger, a believer would draw one arc of the symbol on the ground. If the other person drew the other arc, they both knew that they shared a love for Christ. They could then openly share their faith without fear of persecution.

The Greek word for fish, *ichthus,* forms an acronym for Jesus Christ, God the Son, Savior. From the very beginning of church history, believers recognized Jesus' association with fish and fishing. Read the following passages and write a simple newspaper headline about Christ's connection with the fishing industry.

Mark 1:16-20 _____

Luke 5:3-11 _____

Matthew 13:47-49 _____

_____

Mark 6:30-44 _____

_____

Mark 8:1-9 _____

_____

John 21:1-14 _____

_____

### Answers

**Mark 1:16-20** Jesus Calls Brothers to Fish for Men

**Luke 5:3-11** Jesus Teaches Fishermen How to Fish

**Matthew 13:47-49** Jesus Compares Kingdom to a Fishnet

**Mark 6:30-44** Jesus Breaks Bread and Fish to Feed 5,000

**Mark 8:1-9** Jesus Feeds 4,000 with 7 Loaves and a Few Fish

**John 21:1-14** Jesus Lives and Shows Disciples How to Fish

any association with heathen religious practices. Some groups would travel the roads to collect money for their temples and places of worship.

Observe also the importance that Jesus placed on their work. The disciples were to travel to the villages and preach the Word of God. He fully expected the people to receive them and to show them customary Jewish hospitality. Those places that rejected the words of the disciples subjected themselves to God's judgment. God destroyed Sodom and Gomorrah for their vile sexual practices.

### Exercise: Food!

**Goal:** To emphasize the Lord's ability to supply large needs.

**Procedure:** Obtain a normal lunch from a student or the school cafeteria. List the types and quantity of food for the lunch. Multiply the quantities by five thousand and estimate the total cost and preparation time. Compare the results with Christ's actions. Direct the discussion toward the greatness of Christ's power.

### PRINCIPLES APPLIED

### Ministering to Others

A vital part of growing in your relationship to Christ is learning how to tell others about the Savior. Fear of rejection or of not knowing what to say often stops believers from obeying the Lord in this matter.

The disciples spoke about the kingdom of God and about repenting of sin. You can do the same in many different ways. Giving out gospel tracts is a simple means of witnessing. You can tell someone about your personal testimony of faith in Christ or start a general conversation with someone and then turn the focus to spiritual issues. You might say, "I'm a Christian and if you will give me a few minutes, I would like to tell you about the Lord." Then share verses from the Bible that explain the plan of salvation. Many people use the following verses called the Romans Road to witness for Christ.

Romans 3:23—All are sinful.

Romans 6:23—The penalty for sin is death.

Romans 14:12—God will judge all men.

Romans 5:8—Christ died in our place.

Romans 10:9, 13—People must believe in Christ.

Even today, these cities are a symbol of wickedness and of God's condemnation of sin. Jesus told the disciples that rejection of their preaching was a greater sin than the sin of Sodom and Gomorrah. Men rejected Jesus and they would also reject the disciples.

Christ wanted them to experience every aspect of the work, including its success. Notice in Mark 6:12, 13 that they preached the same message as Christ, and likewise cast out demons and healed the sick. Verse 30 records the return and the report of the disciples. You can almost hear the excited enthusiasm as they "told him **all** things, both what they had done, and what they had taught [emphasis added]."

102

### Exercise: Teachings of Christ

**Goal:** To review the teachings of Christ.

**Procedure:** Divide the class into groups of three or four students. Ask them to list six to ten specific teachings of Christ that the people at the feeding of the four thousand may have heard. Allow the students to use their Bibles and require them to include the references with each item. They may use the other Gospels as needed. Collect the papers for a grade.

# Cooperating in the Ministry I
## Mark 6:30-44

The story of the feeding of the five thousand is very familiar to most of us. But have you ever considered Christ's purpose for this event? Jesus quietly revealed His power as God while allowing the disciples to cooperate in the work and ministry to the masses. We will see again that discipleship is recognizing Christ's person and then following His teaching and direction for our lives.

After the disciples reported to Jesus about their work, He knew that they needed rest. They tried to travel privately by boat to the other side of Galilee, but the multitudes saw them. Some ran around the lake to the other side and met Jesus when the boat arrived. Christ saw their needs and desire for instruction, and He began to teach them.

We can assume that He was probably as tired as the others. Christ's compassion toward human adversity motivated Him to continue. The disciples seem to rebuke Jesus for the long teaching session when they suggested that He send the people away to buy food. His response, "Give ye them to eat," must have startled the disciples. They reasoned that the equivalent of eight months of a laborer's salary would be needed to buy enough bread for all the people. The prospects seemed impossible. By now, we tend to expect the disciples to catch on to the fact that Jesus, as God, was capable of meeting this need. Christ told the twelve to find out how much food was present. The report came back that they had five small loaves of barley bread and two small salted fish, which was about the size of a boy's lunch.

Christ commanded the crowd to sit down in groups of fifty and one hundred so all might be served in an orderly fashion. He then prayed a blessing, broke the bread and fish, and gave them to the disciples for distribution. Right before the disciples' eyes, Jesus multiplied a meager lunch to feed a multitude. Most of the

The Lord often used shepherding terminology to describe the spiritual needs of men. See Numbers 27:17; II Chronicles 18:16; Ezekiel 34:5.

A common laborer would earn about one penny or denarius per day.

Notice Christ's orderliness in feeding the crowd. He had them sit in groups of fifty and one hundred. The disciples served and then gathered the fragments. Jesus then dismissed the people. Everyone had the opportunity to eat because of the organizational structure. Offers of free food on a city street corner or at a ball game can result in mob-like conditions. Many would not be able to get to the food.

crowd probably did not realize what Jesus was doing. The meal was very simple, but it filled them. They were glad for the food and for the teaching. Christ cared for both the physical and spiritual needs of the people. The disciples saw Christ's compassion and His power. He allowed them to participate in the work as they obeyed His directions. The union between the divine Christ and obedient disciples would become the pattern for all spiritual victories.

## *T*eachings on the Sea
### Mark 6:45-54

Jesus' next two lessons for the twelve are similar to previous ones. Some critics of the Bible contend that the same events are recorded twice due to an editorial error. These people fail to understand the nature of the Bible's inspiration and the depravity of the human heart. Christ repeated the teachings because the disciples failed to understand their true significance the first time. You and I likewise seldom comprehend spiritual lessons the first time. Mark adds a comment to the end of this section, which summarizes the real issue. "For they considered not the miracle of the loaves: for their heart was hardened" (Mark 6:52). The Lord expects us to see His working and instruction through His Word and the circumstances of our lives. Followers of Christ often fail their Master. We can be thankful that He will try again to teach us those lessons that elude our understanding. The Lord is merciful to us in our weakness.

Immediately after feeding the masses, Jesus compelled the disciples to leave for the other side of the lake by boat. The word *constrained* indicates that He had to persuade them to leave. Something seems to have aroused the disciples or the crowd. Perhaps the people wanted Jesus to start a revolution against the Romans. Perhaps they just wanted to be fed again. Christ dismissed the people and went to a mountain to pray. Verse 47 signifies that the time was early evening or around 6 P.M. He could clearly see the disciples rowing the boat into a mighty wind toward the other side. By the fourth watch of the night or about 3 A.M., Jesus walked on the water going to the other side. Mark

"As before, at the storm on the lake (cf. chapter iv), the presence of Christ brought peace to the disciples. But their fear then and their amazement here is traced by the Evangelist to their failure to learn the previous lesson of the feeding of the five thousand. Smallness of faith is a failure to consider God's working in the past and to apply that knowledge of His nature to our present problems" (Cole, 116-17).

### George Mueller: Faith in God's Provision

George Mueller (1805-1898) lived a very wicked life while studying for the ministry in Eastern Europe. At a prayer meeting, he repented and believed in Christ. His life changed radically. In time the Lord led him to Bristol, England, to pastor a church and eventually to start numerous ministries for the poor, including several orphanages. Mueller's great faith in God's provision for the physical needs of His people continues to encourage believers today. Mueller believed in asking God alone to provide for the children. He would not appeal to people for money or other necessities. Biographies of Mueller abound with God's answers to his prayers. The following excerpt is from A. T. Pierson, Mueller's son-in-law. In this situation, all funds were depleted and they could look only to God for help. Notice the strong faith of the house parent.

"A gentleman and some ladies visiting the orphan house saw the large number of little ones to be cared for. One of the ladies said to the matron of the Boys' House: 'Of course you cannot carry on these institutions without a good stock of funds'; and the gentleman added, 'Have you a good stock?' The quiet answer was, 'Our funds are deposited in a bank which cannot break.' The reply drew tears from the eyes of the lady, and a gift of five pounds from the pocket of the gentleman—a donation most opportune, as there was not one penny then in hand."

Have you learned the lesson that God can supply for your needs? We should be like David when he cried, "The Lord is my shepherd, I shall not want" (Psalm 23:1).

tells us that Christ "would have passed by them" (Mark 6:48). The disciples' wearisome trial is nothing for the Son of God. The sight of Christ on the water caused the disciples to stop fearing the elements. They now feared Christ. His words of comfort to them again revealed His identity. *It is I* is the Greek expression of the Hebrew name of God revealed to Moses in Exodus 3. When Jesus got into the boat, the wind ceased and the twelve were astonished. The disciples' safety rested in the deity of Christ. True discipleship focuses on the person and work of God's Son.

## Cooperating in the Ministry II
### Mark 8:1-9

The feeding of the four thousand is another very familiar story to us. Differences from the feeding of the five thousand include the number of people present, the amount of food at the beginning and at the end, and the type of vessel used to store the gathered fragments. In Mark 6, the disciples used small lunch pouches, which were generally carried around the waist. This time, they used larger baskets that may have stored fish.

Jesus makes His two purposes for this event very clear to us. The multitude had been listening to Him teach for three days without the opportunity to obtain food. Some of the people had probably brought provisions with them, but even their supply was now exhausted. Jesus simply wanted to show compassion for their physical needs. Most of us would not endure three days of spiritual instruction without focusing on food.

Observe Jesus' second purpose as He presents the problem to the disciples. He expects them to believe that He is able to provide the food. Just a few months before, they had seen Him feed an even larger crowd. Their answer in Mark 8:4 shows that they still looked to human wisdom as a means of meeting men's needs. The twelve stood in the presence of God's Son, but did not comprehend His ability to solve the problem. Jesus wanted to show them His power once again that they might recognize Him. He took the food, blessed it, broke it, and gave it to the disciples for distribution to the people. This time, they gathered seven large baskets of leftovers. Jesus probably used the larger baskets and larger quantity of fragments as a visual lesson for the disciples. Who else but God could multiply a small lunch into such abundance?

A very short time later (Mark 8:10-21), the Pharisees asked Jesus for a sign of His authority and He refused to give one to them. He then got into a boat with the disciples and warned them

Christ's rebuke of the disciples in Mark 8:10-21 clearly shows that He expected them to learn spiritual lessons from His supplying their physical needs. God does not intend to use every minor detail of life to teach us profound lessons. True disciples, however, will be able to see God's hand in their lives through the Word and through the circumstances of life.

---

### Review: Crossword Puzzle

**Goal:** To review people and events in the Gospel of Mark.

**Procedure:** See the crossword puzzle in the Appendix (pp. 157-58). The assignment may be used for class work, homework, or extra credit. Grade the work to encourage student accountability.

about the doctrine of the religious leaders. The warning came in the form of a figure of speech about leaven, which symbolized sin. The disciples thought that Jesus was concerned about their lack of bread on the boat. He chastised them for not learning that He could supply all the bread they needed. Christ's main concern was spiritual. The disciples saw only the physical. Even after a second lesson, the disciples failed to understand the person and power of Christ.

## Training for Discipleship
### Mark 8:27–9:1

Jesus now deliberately led the disciples away from the crowds around Galilee toward Caesarea Philippi. He needed a quieter place to privately teach the twelve some very important concepts about Himself and about life. As they walked along, He asked them who other people thought He might be. The group had certainly heard chatter about Him in the marketplaces and synagogues. Their answers revealed that the Jews regarded Jesus as a great man. Some superstitiously thought that He was John the Baptist raised from the dead.

Jesus then focused the disciples' attention on the real issue by asking what they thought. Peter answered correctly by proclaiming that Jesus was the Christ or the Messiah. All the months of

# THOU ART THE CHRIST

teaching, observation, and work finally came to fruition. But their concept of the Messiah was flawed. Like most Jews, they expected a political kingdom that would restore national sovereignty to Israel. Jesus revealed to them that He would die at the hands of the religious leadership in Jerusalem. Three days later, He would rise from the dead.

Peter decided to correct the Lord's thinking by talking to Him away from the others. Jesus' words probably never left Peter's mind. "Get thee behind me, Satan: for thou savourest not the

107

Christ patiently teaches the twelve one step at a time. First they must recognize His identity. Now they must understand the true nature of the Messiah. Jesus begins directing their thoughts to His death. See Mark 9:12, 31, 32; 10:32-34.

The Greek verb tenses in Mark 8:34 aid our understanding of Christ's teaching on discipleship decisions. *Deny* and *take* are both aorists. The aorist tense indicates simple action, not continuous activity. Most commentators believe that these are one-time decisions. On the other hand, *follow* is in the present tense, indicating continuous action. The disciple comes to a point in life where he decides to deny self and to identify with Christ. He then follows Christ on a daily basis.

Notice the emphasis in the passage on the future life. Jesus would rise on the third day. Disciples who lose their lives would find them at a future time. Man can lose his soul and the entire world cannot purchase it.

Part of the teacher's task is to nurture the student's faith just as Christ did with His twelve disciples. The process will take years of patient instruction. A wise teacher will discern the student's spiritual condition and direct the learning process

---

## Discussion: The World Versus Christ

**Goal:** To draw distinction between Christ and the world.

**Procedure:** Divide the class into three groups. Assign to each group one of the topics listed below. The group has fifteen minutes to develop a five-minute presentation about the topic for the rest of the class. Emphasize that believers must make a clean break with the world to follow Christ. Those

who try to please both sides are utterly miserable.

1. What does the Bible say about the conflict between Christians and the world?

2. Why do people in the world oppose Christians?

3. What symbols or examples represent the world's opposition to Christ?

**107**

accordingly. Discipleship requires an increasing awareness
of Christ's power and deity.
Believers will make life-altering
decisions required for discipleship when they begin to comprehend the majesty of Christ.

things that be of God, but the things that be of men" (Mark 8:33).
Jesus corrected Peter's thinking. God's will was for Jesus to die in
the place of sinners. Christ would then secure eternal life for His
people. The political kingdom would come much later. Jesus'
words to Peter were very strong. Peter needed to understand the
entire truth about the person of Christ, and so must all of His
disciples. We may not fully comprehend the depths of Christ's
person and work, but we must accept them as truth.

Jesus then began to instruct them
about the true nature of discipleship.
Christ expounds three requirements;
they teach us that a true disciple
will follow the steps of His master. First, disciples must deny
themselves. At the very heart of
sin is the desire to put self first.
Adam and Eve acted out of self-
interest when they ate the fruit in
Eden. Satan convinced Eve that
God withheld something good from
them and that they could gain it back by
disobedience to God's clear command. Jesus
certainly denied Himself by coming to earth to die for sinners.

Second, a disciple must take up the cross. The Jews were very
familiar with the cross as a form of execution and torture. The
Romans did everything possible to make shameful examples of
those who defied their law. Jesus would suffer on a cross for
doing the will of God. Disciples must likewise understand that
the world is antagonistic toward God. Those who follow Christ
must willingly accept the reproach of the world.

Third, the disciple of Christ must follow Christ. The verb *follow* is in the present tense indicating that the action is continuous.
Believers do the things that Jesus did.

The cost of discipleship is very high. Logically, we may won-
der why anyone would want to meet Christ's conditions for following Him. Jesus anticipated the question and proceeded to give
several answers which focus on eternal values.

108

### Exercise: How Can You Follow Christ?

**Goal:** To encourage specific efforts to follow Christ.

**Procedure:** Divide the blackboard into five sections. Write one of the follow-ing items in each section: self-denial, compassion, fellowship with God, evangelism, and discipleship. Ask the students to think of one specific way that they can presently follow Christ in each area. Allow the students to write their ideas on the board. Discuss the results of each category. Emphasize that they can follow Christ.

First, in Mark 8:35, Jesus clearly states that those who act to save their current lives will actually lose their lives. The opposite is also true. Those who lose their lives will gain them. Christ willingly lost His life for our sakes and then gained it back at His Resurrection. Believers can expect to do the same.

Second, nothing compares to the value of the soul. Man cannot buy his life with all the goods in the world. Therefore, losing your life to gain eternal life is a great bargain.

Third, a day of great judgment is coming. A person's relationship to Christ and to the world will be the basis of judgment. Those who deny Christ to gain favor with the world will suffer great loss.

## Some Final Thoughts

Jesus taught the disciples many lessons. Keep in mind that the twelve were almost always present as Christ healed the sick, cast out demons, preached to the crowds, and rebuked the religious leaders. He also sent them out to work alone. They often failed to understand His lessons. We might be tempted to give them a poor grade for substandard performance. Being a disciple of Christ means that we have a close and energetic relationship with Him. What lessons is Jesus teaching you today? Do you increasingly recognize Him as God? Would He give you a passing grade as a disciple?

109

## Discussion: Disciple Stoppers

**Goal:** To inform students about common hindrances to discipleship in their school, church, or circle of friends.

**Procedure:** Ask the class to tell you why people don't follow Christ. Be prepared to point out the temporal nature of the reasons.

# Review Questions

__F__ 1. Jesus called James and John to leave their fishing business in the first year of His ministry.

__F__ 2. *Apostle* means "to follow."

__F__ 3. The Sea of Galilee is six hundred feet above sea level.

__F__ 4. The Old Testament required four witnesses to verify the truthfulness of a testimony or claim.

__T__ 5. Gomorrah is a symbol of wickedness.

__F__ 6. The fourth watch of the night started at 10 p.m.

__T__ 7. The disciples gathered seven baskets of leftovers at the feeding of the four thousand.

__F__ 8. Jesus stopped teaching the disciples when they recognized Him as God.

__F__ 9. Jesus taught the disciples that Messiah would die in Galilee.

__T__ 10. A man's soul is worth more than all the money in the world.

11. Compare or contrast how Jesus' death paralleled His requirements for being a disciple.

*Jesus set aside His own comforts and interests to die for sinners. Disciples must deny self-interest to follow Christ.*

12. Why did Jesus not choose His disciples from the religious leadership in Jerusalem?

*Jesus did not choose any of the religious leaders because they rejected His teaching almost from the beginning. The men He chose responded eagerly to His word.*

13. What did Jesus do to help the disciples' credibility as they ministered in the villages in Mark 6:7-13?

*Jesus gave them power over unclean spirits so that people might believe their preaching. He also sent them out in pairs and commanded them not to adopt the methods of heathen religions.*

111

14. Why did Jesus walk on the water in Mark 6:45-54?

*Jesus walked on the water to show the disciples that He was God. The disciples would then focus on Christ and not on the circumstances around them.*

15. How can a person lose his life by saving it?

*A person who tries to hold onto his present sinful life and lifestyle will not be prepared for eternity. He will lose eternal life by trying to retain the present.*

# CHAPTER SEVEN

# Christ and the Disciples—Part II
### 7

Ten guys and girls sat in the new ice cream parlor near the school. Third quarter exams were now completed, and the teachers planned to post grades in two days. Normally, the "lunch crew," as they called themselves, would celebrate the end of exams by getting together for a short party. The tradition included a strict rule about not discussing tests and projects. But this time, the discussion centered on Mr. Franklin's long essay questions in English literature. Everybody's answers seemed to be different. Several worried out loud about the potential effect the test might have on the report cards. The "lunch crew" had been together in school since third grade and could well empathize with each other's situations.

Jerry spoke up, "It seems to me that we are straying from our tradition of trying to forget about exams. Let's all get ice cream cones this time and talk about anything other than Milton and Shakespeare."

The server came and patiently took each order. Anna was the last one to decide which flavor she wanted.

Anna finally said, "I will take cherry chocolate chip in a cone. Could you please include a spoon with mine?"

Cindy asked, "Who ever heard of someone eating an ice cream cone with a spoon? I thought cones were for licking!"

Everyone, including Anna, just laughed. The conversation quickly returned to the school year and to graduation. Soon, the servers returned with ten huge ice cream cones and Anna's spoon.

### Goals

Students should

1. Recognize the deity of Christ in Mark's Gospel.
2. Understand faith and obedience in discipleship.
3. Recognize indications of failure in discipleship.
4. Focus on Christ's work.
5. Evaluate their personal lives for potential failure.
6. Establish a vital relationship to Christ.

### Objectives

Students should be able to

1. State specific indications of Christ's deity from Mark.
2. Explain the roles of faith and obedience in discipleship.
3. Use standard tools and methods for effective Bible study.
4. Explain the basic significance of Christ's death and Resurrection.

### Scripture Reading

1. Mark 9-16
2. John 18-21

### Memory Verses

1. Mark 9:7
2. Mark 14:22-24

113

## Lecture Overview

### Introduction

1. Recognizing key themes in Mark is an important Bible study skill.
2. The deity of Christ leads to Christian discipleship.

### The Transfiguration

1. Jesus is God's Son.
2. Jesus planned to die for sinners.

### Christ Teaches About His Death

1. Recognizing repetitive grammar is an important Bible study skill.
2. Jesus describes His death to the disciples.

### Dangers for the Disciples

1. Christians may lose their effectiveness.
2. Service to others must replace personal ambition.
3. Supporting others must replace petty sectarianism.
4. Edifying others must replace personal desires.

### Lessons with the King

1. Obedience leads to growth.
2. Jesus presented Himself as Messiah to the Jews.
3. Jesus judged wicked religious practices.
4. Jesus encouraged faith in God.

**Lesson Plans**

**Day 1** Class reading of Mark

Homework: Read Student Text Chapter 7

**Day 2** Introduction, The Transfiguration, Christ Teaches About His Death, Dangers for the Disciples, Lessons with the King lecture

**Day 3** Verbs exercise

**Day 4** Communion with Christ, The School of Failure, Knowing Christ lecture

**Day 5** Great Statements worksheet

**Thoughts for the Teacher**

1. Remember that reading the text of Mark will significantly affect the students. See the Appendix (p. 134) for ideas.

2. God will bless a teacher's fervent prayer for the success of the Word with the students.

3. Every lecture and activity must be focused on the establishment of a vital relationship to Christ.

4. Avoid any drift toward exalting failure. Our task is to vaccinate against failure, not to encourage it.

5. Remember that much of what the students will gain is "caught and not taught." They must see examples of discipleship and genuine love for Christ. They will certainly see the failures and the hypocrites. Your life must show the reality of knowing Christ. The formal teaching of Mark's Gospel is only one part of the battle.

After three or four satisfying licks on the ice cream cones, almost everyone noticed Anna's technique. She carefully dug through the vanilla ice cream with the spoon to extract the cherries and chocolate chips, which she delightedly ate. Every minute or two, she would lick the vanilla to find more cherries.

Anna noticed the attention and slyly said, "Yes, I'm different! Mr. Franklin said in English class that a good way to analyze an author is to find one or two key themes and to look for them in the literature. It worked well in class. I thought I would try it with ice cream. The key themes today are cherries and chocolate chips! My essay thesis will be 'Frozen cherries are delicious'!"

Larry replied, "The cold ice cream probably got into the cherries to make them taste better, but they're not frozen anymore. Just look at the puddle of vanilla on the table and on your hand."

Anna quickly abandoned her spoon and began eating in earnest.

Our "ice cream cone" is our study of Mark's Gospel. The cherries are Christ's relationships with various groups of people. His power and compassion should give us a great foundation for living in this world. Much of Jesus' work focused on training the twelve disciples. In the last chapter, we saw Him patiently revealing His deity to them. Knowledge always brings responsibility. The disciples knew that Jesus was the Messiah; now they must learn to follow Him. In this chapter we will see Jesus patiently explaining to the twelve what it means to be a follower or a disciple. He will also show them through His example. At times, we might consider Christ's requirements to be difficult. The disciples constantly saw Jesus' power. They knew that He was God. When we focus on Christ's person and power as God, the requirements for discipleship will be delightful. Anna used a spoon to dig cherries and chocolate chips out of her vanilla ice cream. We will use our Bible study skills to "dig out" teachings on Christ's deity and our discipleship from the last months of Jesus' time on earth.

114

## Communion with Christ

1. Obedience leads to growth.
2. Remembering Christ's death leads to discipleship.

## The School of Failure

1. Unbelief and disobedience lead to failure.
2. Failure has many symptoms.
3. Christ forgives and restores.

## Knowing Christ

1. Jesus is God's Son.
2. Man is weak and sinful.
3. Knowing Christ is the basis of all life.

## Discussion: Digging for Treasure

**Goal:** To consider the need for great effort to find valuable items.

**Procedure:** Find the following items or equivalents: gold ring, gemstone, motor oil, sale item, antiques. Ask the students to tell you what the items have in common. Point out that obtaining the items required some type of digging and great effort. Emphasize that finding Bible truths requires the

## The Transfiguration
### Mark 9:1-13

Peter's great confession about Jesus' being the Messiah was simply the introduction to several teachings that must have startled the disciples. Jesus told them that He would die. If they wanted to be His disciples, they must follow the same path of self-denial. Christ rose from the dead, and similarly the disciples would also enjoy the benefits of a new life. The Jews' concept of the Messiah was much different. They looked for a political and military leader.

Jesus took Peter, James, and John to an isolated mountain to teach them about His deity and the truthfulness of His teachings. Mark 9:2 tells us that Jesus was "transfigured" or "metamorphosed." Most will recognize the word from a study of biology. It means to change into another form, just as a caterpillar changes into a butterfly. Mark emphasizes that this change was not of human origin. No man could have made Jesus' shining clothing. Peter, James, and John saw Jesus in His glorified body. He was God and He was human. They also saw Moses and Elijah talking to Jesus. Moses represented the law while Elijah represented the prophets. Both wrote about Christ. Luke's Gospel tells us that they spoke about Jesus' death.

Out of fear, Peter asked Jesus if he could build three tents, presumably for prolonging the experience. God the Father then spoke to the group from a cloud, "This is my beloved Son: hear him." God identified Jesus as His Son and also validated the lessons that Christ taught the disciples. Remember that the Old Testament required two or three witnesses to confirm the truthfulness of a claim. Peter, James, and John had now heard from three great witnesses that Jesus was God and that He would die for sinners.

As the four departed from the mountain, Jesus told them not to tell anyone about the experience until He was risen from the dead. They failed to understand the Resurrection, but feared to ask Him about it. Rather, they asked about a less important issue regarding the scribes' teaching on Elijah. They believed that

One of the primary lessons taught by the account of the Transfiguration depends heavily upon the historical context of the events. Jesus' announcement of His death probably shocked the disciples. The Gospel of Mark contains many instances in which the disciples simply did not understand. The Transfiguration then became more than a display of Christ's deity. It was a confirmation that His words about His death were true. Always encourage an examination of the context in order to interpret a passage of Scripture properly.

The Jews believed that Moses wrote about Christ. See John 1:45 and Deuteronomy 18:15.

The Jews also believed that Elijah would precede the appearance of the Messiah. See Malachi 3:1 and 4:5.

See Deuteronomy 17:6 and 19:15 for the required number of witnesses.

The best interpretation of Mark 9:12 seems to be to regard *how it is written of Him* as a question. The Greek documents did not contain punctuation marks.

same. Only those who work to obtain the truth will find the truth.

### Exercise: Term Review
**Goal:** To review key terms in the Gospel of Mark.

**Procedure:** Write the terms listed below on the chalkboard. Ask each student to write down a definition of each word. Allow several students to share their definitions with the class.

Jesus: "Jehovah saves"; personal name of God's Son

Christ: Greek equivalent of the Hebrew word *Messiah*

Messiah: "Anointed"; The Messiah was God's promised deliverer.

Disciple: Follower

Apostle: One sent on a mission

Deity: The nature and character of being God

### Exercise: Change
**Goal:** To illustrate Christ's change at the Transfiguration.

**Procedure:** Divide the class into four groups. Assign each group one of the following items: caterpillar, tadpole, flour and yeast, wrecked car. Ask the groups to describe the process required to transform their item into a butterfly, frog, bread, or a usable car. Then ask them to contrast their item's process with Christ's transfiguration.

Elijah would reappear before the coming of Messiah. Jesus told them that Elijah had already appeared. He referred to the ministry of John the Baptist, which the religious leaders rejected. More importantly, Jesus focused their attention back on His death and suffering. The second part of Mark 9:12 should be punctuated as a question. Jesus was trying to direct their minds away from secondary issues so that they might concentrate on His death.

## Christ Teaches About His Death
### Mark 9:30-32; 10:32-34

On at least two occasions in the weeks prior to His death, Jesus taught the disciples about His death. The length of the recorded teaching probably does not reflect the actual time Jesus spent on the subject. *Taught* in Mark 9:31 is in the imperfect tense, indicating that the action was continuous or not complete. The group walked from around Caesarea Philippi to Capernaum, a trip of about forty miles, which would take at least two days. Jesus had ample opportunity to speak to the twelve on the road or during breaks for meals. They could then think about His words as they walked.

Notice the specifics of Jesus' teaching. He would be delivered into the hands of men. *Deliver* is a passive form meaning that someone else would deliver Jesus. The subject is not definite. It may be that Jesus referred to the betrayal of Judas. More likely, He

The Christ of Derision, *by Philippe de Champaigne, Bob Jones University Collection*

116

Christ's foreknowledge of His death is the basis of His pronouncements to the disciples. This points to His deity and control of the situation.

In Mark 10:32, Christ "went before" or led the disciples to Jerusalem. Hiebert notes that this was not the normal walking with the disciples but actually leading them to the city (Hiebert, 295).

Note also the group went *up* to Jerusalem. To the Jews, movement towards Jerusalem was "up" and movement away was "down." This distinction came partly from the geographical height of the city and also from the Jews' belief that Jerusalem was the center of all worship and life.

---

Direct the discussion toward the purpose and miraculous nature of Christ's transfiguration.

### Discussion: Where Are We?

**Goal:** To focus on indications that Christ planned to die.

**Procedure:** Show the class a map of a road heading toward an ocean or a lake. Ask them to list things that would indicate to them as they drove that they were getting near the water.

Examples may include road signs, sand, sea gulls, and gift shops. Ask the class to tell you how the disciples might know that Jesus was going to die. Examples include Christ's teaching, the hostility of the Jewish leaders, Christ's travel to Jerusalem, and OT Scriptures.

### Discussion: Repetition in Learning

**Goal:** To illustrate the reason Jesus repeated teachings and teaching methods.

**Procedure:** On your board or overhead write the following phrases: *music lessons, football practice, school curriculum, and dog obedience school.* Ask the class to tell you why each activity uses repetition as an aid to learning. Discuss why Jesus often repeated

## Bible Study Techniques

**TEXT TOOLS**

A great way to study the Bible is to write a one-sentence summary about the main teaching of a chapter or paragraph. This method can be difficult at first, but it gets easier with practice. Successful athletes work hard at perfecting their skills over time. Christians should do the same. Use the following steps as a guide.

1. Choose a short paragraph or section.

2. Read the passage at least ten times.

3. Use a dictionary to look up unfamiliar words.

4. Notice any repetitive words or ideas.

5. List the main characters and their roles in the incident.

6. Try to determine why the Lord included this passage in the Bible.

7. Decide upon the main subject of the passage and express it in one or two words. Examples include sin, faith, repentance, God's love, etc.

8. Write a simple sentence on what the passage teaches about the subject. Example: Man must repent in order to enter the kingdom.

9. Determine whether the sentence accurately reflects the intent of the text by rereading the passage several times.

10. Revise the sentence as needed.

---

spoke of God the Father's plan regarding the role of the religious leaders in Christ's death. Peter probably recalled Jesus' teaching when he preached on the day of Pentecost in Acts 2. "Him, being delivered by the determinate counsel and foreknowledge of God, ye have taken, and by wicked hands have crucified and slain" (Acts 2:23). Notice too that Jesus twice used the word *kill* to describe what would happen in Jerusalem. Again, the disciples failed to understand and were afraid to ask (Mark 9:32).

Later, Jesus led the disciples to Jerusalem (Mark 10:32-34). Their fear and amazement indicates that they knew what was likely to happen. Perhaps they believed His words, but simply

117

---

His teachings. Emphasize that our sinful hearts are often unresponsive to spiritual truth. Point out that God mercifully repeats lessons so that we may understand and believe.

### Exercise: Verbs

**Goal:** To clarify the meaning of Scripture by using a dictionary.

**Procedure:** Divide the class into groups of two or three students. Instruct each group to read Mark 10:33, 34 and to list the seven verbs about Christ's passion. Look up each word in an English dictionary, Strong's concordance, or a theological dictionary. Have the students write the definitions and then find the verses in Mark that record the actual event that Christ spoke about. Emphasize Christ's foreknowledge, which points to His deity.

could not comprehend all that He said. The fact that Jesus again explicitly told them what would happen points to His knowledge as God. He both knew the situation and controlled the situation. This created real fear in the disciples, but later, it would be a great comfort. The death of their Master was not an accident. He planned to die for them. Notice that Jesus used eight verbs to describe the events in Jerusalem. The final one should give them hope during the trials that lay ahead. Jesus would rise from the dead. They simply needed to believe and to trust in all that Jesus said.

## Dangers for the Disciples
### Mark 9:33-50

Immediately following the second of Jesus' teachings about His death, the disciples argued about which one of them would be the greatest in the kingdom. They thought that Jesus did not know about the conflict and seemed to be embarrassed when He asked them about it (Mark 9:34). Christ took this problem as an opening to discuss many dangers that the disciples currently faced and would face to an even greater extent in the future. But, in order to understand Jesus' intention, we need to examine His conclusion before we look at each potential problem.

One well-respected Bible scholar believes that Mark 9:49 and 50 are the two hardest verses in the New Testament to interpret (Hiebert, 269). Our western thought patterns are not like those in the ancient Near East. The best we can do is capture the essence of the meaning; some of the details and logic will elude us. The verses start with the word *for,* which tells us that Jesus is drawing a conclusion to the entire section. Salt was commonly used in Palestine as a preservative. Its necessity for life made salt a valuable commodity. Some ancient cultures used it in treaties as a symbol of good intentions or genuineness. The disciples would also recognize it as a necessary part of Old Testament sacrifices. Salt therefore seems to point to the purification and veracity of a relationship.

Foreign missionaries will readily attest to the fact that people in other cultures think differently. Part of effective Bible study is learning to extract the principle from the cultural setting.

See the following verses on salt: Leviticus 2:13; Numbers 18:19; and II Chronicles 13:5.

118

Jesus makes a connection between salt and fire in verse 49. John the Baptist preached that Jesus would baptize people with the Holy Spirit and fire (Matt. 3:11). An Old Testament believer would see salt as a symbol of a relationship with God. The New Testament believer would see fire in the same manner. In verse 50, Jesus says that the believer's effectiveness can be lost just as salt can lose its taste. Jesus implies that wrongful dealings with others can spoil our effectiveness in the kingdom. The power and purifying aspects of our relationship to God must spill over to our dealings with other believers. Jesus gives us three interconnected categories of danger that can ruin our service to God and our relationships to others.

First, personal ambition has no place in God's kingdom (Mark 9:34-37). Jesus answered the disciples' question about who should be greatest by exalting service. The greatest would be the servant. Jesus served God, and He also served the disciples in numerous ways. They should do the same. Notice too that the object of the service must include those who are weakest and most vulnerable in the kingdom. Jesus saw the child's innocent faith. The disciples must receive children. Instead of exalting self, a true disciple will serve those who respond to Christ.

Second, petty divisions among believers have no place in God's kingdom (Mark 9:38-41). The disciples stopped a man who was casting out unclean spirits in Jesus' name. Christ's words and actions made deep divisions among the Jews. Those who hated Jesus would logically not do anything to further His cause. The others, however, responded to Christ—as evidenced by their actions. The disciples must not do

The word *servant* in Mark 9:35 is translated "deacon" in Philippians 1:1 and I Timothy 3:8.

A person's relationship to Christ is the real issue in Mark 9:38-41. Inclusion in a specific group is not a test of fellowship. Mature believers will see beyond labels and affiliations. Those who genuinely love Christ and obediently work for Him must not be hindered. This does not give credence to ecumenism, which denies the basic doctrines of Scripture to pursue religious unity. Christ powerfully denounced false religion and so must we.

119

---

### Discussion: Why Do People Want to Be Great?

**Goal:** To emphasize the need for Christ's teaching about being a servant.

**Procedure:** Ask the students to state several reasons that teens want to be great. Write them on the chalkboard. Examples include the desire for attention, power, wealth, possessions, and many others. Further ask how these teens may act at school, work, or church. Point out that each attitude and action comes from a selfish heart. Contrast the selfishness with Christ's call to be a servant.

### Exercise: Assisting the Work

**Goal:** To increase awareness of opportunities to serve God.

**Procedure:** Enlist the aid of a pastor or other Christian leader in speaking to the class about service opportunities for teens. Introduce the session by giving the pastor a glass of cold water. Explain that God will reward even such a small gesture of kindness. After the session, emphasize that teens should not be jealous of or discourage the efforts of others who may be serving God in a different capacity or in another location.

anything to extinguish the active faith of others. God commended the efforts of those who would do something as small as giving a cup of water. They must likewise commend the efforts of others who work for Christ.

Third, actions that lead to sin have no place in God's kingdom (Mark 9:42-48). The Greek word *offend* means much more than doing something that annoys or embarrasses. It means "to stumble" or "to cause to sin." Notice that Jesus first applies the principle to children or, by interpretation, those who respond but are weak. The disciple must ever be careful to nurture and not destroy the faith of others. Jesus also applies it to personal issues. Cutting off the hand or foot is a figure of speech. Anything that might hinder our entrance into the kingdom must be terminated. The disciple must therefore guard his own faith to ensure a positive response to Christ.

## *L*essons with the King
### Mark 11:1-26

Jesus now approached the city of Jerusalem. The time was short, and the disciples still required much training. They needed to concentrate on Christ's deity and on His expectation for them. The twelve would then be ready to face His humiliation and death. Jesus taught them a lesson in basic discipleship. He commanded two of them to go into a nearby village to obtain a colt. He also told them how to answer anyone who asked why they were taking the colt. As God, He knew the animal's location and

120

## Discussion: Causing Others to Sin

**Goal:** To encourage living for the benefit of others.

**Procedure:** Read the following story to the students and ask them how they might respond to the situation. Alter the story to make it more applicable to the specific group of students. Emphasize that others may interpret our actions differently than we intend.

Jason's unsaved older brother Steve asked him to pick up a case of beer and a package of cigarettes at the grocery store when doing errands for their mother. Steve worked on the family car and did not have time to do any shopping. Jason bought the items along with the things their mother needed. A few weeks later, Jason asked some of his classmates to come to a church activity to hear about Christ. One friend had seen Jason buy the beer and cigarettes. He refused to come to the church activity. The friend

thought that Jason was just like everyone else and that his religion was a waste of time.

that the owners would release it to the disciples. They found the animal just as Jesus said. Christ's words were completely trustworthy. Obedience led to a better appreciation of His greatness.

Jesus rode the donkey toward the city. The Old Testament prophets had spoken of Messiah's entry into the city on a donkey (Zech. 9:9). People visiting Jerusalem for the Passover celebration now came out to welcome Jesus. They spread clothing and tree branches in the road as He passed by. Others joined in a procession to the city. All cried out, "Hosanna: Blessed is he that cometh in the name of the Lord." The disciples would know that the cry was a quote from Psalm 118 about the Messiah. Jesus did not restrain the crowds. He publicly presented Himself as their Messiah and King.

Laying palm branches in the road was a gesture and welcome to people of high rank.

*Hosanna* means "save now."

Jesus spent the night outside Jerusalem in the small village of Bethany. The visiting crowds praised Jesus as Messiah, but the religious leadership viewed Him differently. Bethany offered a safe haven for rest. The next day He returned to the temple to display His authority as King. You will remember that the priests sold animals for sacrifice and exchanged foreign coins within and around the temple. Their corrupt practices were well known in the ancient world. Jesus overturned the tables of money and expelled the merchants. He further quoted from the prophets to explain His actions to the multitude. The priests had turned the temple into a robber's den. God intended it to be a place where He could meet His people. Jesus the Messiah was simply restoring God's original purpose for this holy place. The disciples saw Jesus' zeal to do the will of God and to judge wicked religion. Only fear of the crowds prevented the scribes and priests from immediately destroying Jesus.

Jesus combined Isaiah 56:7 and Jeremiah 7:11 in denouncing the religious leaders' temple practices.

See Luke 18:10; Acts 3:1; and Acts 16:13 for the association between the temple and prayer.

121

### Discussion: Teen Zeal

**Goal:** To encourage active righteousness in teens.

**Procedure:** Act out Christ's actions as He overturned the moneychangers' tables and drove out the merchants from the Temple. Point out Christ's zeal to do God's will. Ask how a teen can act zealously for God.

The Lord had one other private lesson for the disciples (Mark 11:12-14, 20-26). Jesus was hungry and saw a fig tree near the road. Upon examination, He found no figs on the tree, and so He said that no one would ever eat from the tree again. Christ judged the tree for a lack of fruit. Many theologians see a parallel to Christ's judgment on the nation of Israel for lack of response to His teaching. The next day as they walked along the same path, Peter saw that the tree was withered from the roots upward. Peter's amazement shows his lack of faith in Christ's words. This time, Jesus moved to the very heart of Peter's problem by encouraging him to "Have faith in God" (Mark 11:22). Mountain moving was a common figure of speech. The Jews used it to refer to God's power. Jesus told them that anything was possible for those who believe God and who forgive their fellow man.

## Communion with Christ
### Mark 14:12-25

Personal fellowship with Christ is perhaps the most important aspect of discipleship. Without it, our spiritual lives dry up, leaving the shell of dead religion. Jesus actively sought for this time of communion. The Passover meal was a high point in the Jewish religious year. Eating this special meal together was a symbol of His close relationship with the disciples. His instructions to two of the disciples about where to prepare the Passover are similar to His words regarding finding the donkey. Jesus described a specific set of circumstances. Women generally carried water. Therefore, the two disciples could easily identify the right man since he would have a pitcher of water. Mark records that they "found as he had said unto them" (Mark 14:16), which indicates that the disciples believed that Jesus' words were more than mere coincidence. As deity, He directed them to the appointed place

See Exodus 12 for the first observance of Passover.

Several commentators suspect that this Passover observance took place in Mark's home.

122

## Worksheet: Great Statements in Mark

**Goal:** To review Mark's Gospel.

**Procedure:** Divide the class into groups of two or three students. Give each group the Great Statements in Mark worksheet in the Appendix (pp. 159-62). Grade the worksheet for completeness and effort.

and gave them the job of preparing the meal. As disciples, they obeyed the Master's direction and worked accordingly.

The actual preparation probably took most of the day. They followed the Jewish ritual of removing any trace of leaven from the house, and they also procured the food. At evening, Jesus and the disciples came to the house and started the ceremonial meal. Jesus told the twelve that one of them was a traitor. One by one they asked Him, "Is it I?" The grammatical form indicates that the asker expected a negative response. Almost every follower of Christ passes through periods of doubt, which are indications of a tender heart. Jesus knew Judas Iscariot's intentions. Mark 14:21 may have been Christ's final offer of mercy to Judas. Most Bible scholars believe that at this time Judas departed from the room.

Jesus then instituted what we know as the Lord's Supper or communion (Mark 14:22-26). His words placed new significance on the bread and wine, which were parts of the traditional Passover observance. The bread symbolized Christ's body. He explained the wine as "my blood of the new testament, which is shed for many." In the Old Testament, Moses sealed the relationship between God and the people by sprinkling blood upon them (Exod. 24:8 ff.). God granted cleansing from sin through the blood of a sacrifice (Lev. 17:11). Additionally, through the prophet Jeremiah, God had promised that a new covenant would eventually replace the old one. Believers would have God's Word in their hearts, and they would enjoy close fellowship with Him (Jer. 31:31-34). Jesus taught the disciples that His death would establish the new covenant. His blood sealed their relationship with God. By consuming the symbolic bread and wine, the disciples showed their agreement with God's purposes for Christ's ministry and death. Christ commanded the disciples to regularly observe this simple meal as a remembrance of Him (Luke 22:19). Followers of Christ find their greatest joy and strength in remembering the Savior.

Doubt is common among those who are close to the Lord. See Matthew 11:1-6 for John the Baptist's doubts and Christ's response. Doubt will drive a godly person to self-examination and greater determination to find God. The wicked often have no fears concerning spiritual issues. See Psalm 123.

For other NT references to the Lord's Supper, see Acts 2:42-47; 20:7; and I Corinthians 10:16-22; 11:20-34.

123

## Discussion: The Instruments of Agreement

**Goal:** To teach the nature of a covenant.

**Procedure:** Ask the students to quickly list five types of business agreements. Examples include sports contracts, credit card purchases, installment loans, cash purchases, and mortgage loans. Identify the instrument of the agreement for each one. Note that all are legally binding once signed by the users. Point out that the binding instrument for our salvation is the new covenant ratified by the blood of Christ.

## *T*he School of Failure

Military leaders know from history and from experience that battles bring to light the integrity of an army. Christ's trial and crucifixion would severely test the disciples' character. Their utter failures would give Christ the opportunity to show them His gracious compassion. The disciples would never be the same.

Following the Lord's Supper, Jesus led the band to the Mount of Olives. He announced that all eleven would depart from Him that very evening. He quoted from Zechariah 13:7 to reinforce the reality of their weakness. Peter and the others affirmed that they would never leave. Remember that all asked, "Is it I?" when Jesus told them about the traitor. Now they refused to hear Christ's words and the Old Testament Scriptures. Jesus told Peter that he would deny Him three times before the rooster crowed twice in the morning. Again, Peter hardened himself and vehemently refused to believe His Master's warning.

Next, Jesus went to the garden of Gethsemane to pray for grace and strength. He separated Peter, James, and John from the others to accompany Him to a secluded place. His struggles at this point would be private, except for the three who were to act as guards. As Jesus prayed, they went to sleep. He woke them up and returned to prayer only to find them asleep again. Jesus woke them up a second and a third time. "Couldest not thou watch one hour?" (Mark 14:37) was a stiff rebuke for someone who had just affirmed his loyalty unto death. Peter could not even discipline his body's need for sleep for an hour of prayer.

This chapter seeks to interpret the events of Mark in the light of Christ's deity and to explore discipleship issues. Looking for a particular theme will often yield excellent results. The section on Christ's trial, death, and Resurrection contains many potential topics. Prayer, submission to God, and God's power are examples of subjects that provide significant insight.

Encourage the students to study the Scriptures with a particular topic in mind. It will make them more alert and responsive to the Word.

## Learning from Christ Today

**PRINCIPLES APPLIED**

The disciples often listened to Jesus Christ as they walked from one place to another. He actively sought times to teach them away from the noisy crowds. Jesus wants the same opportunity with us. Living for Christ means learning how to fellowship with Him daily through personal devotions. Use the following suggestions to guide your communication with the Savior.

1. Read the Bible: Ask God to teach you something that you need that day, and then systematically read through the Bible. Bible reading schedules are available from the Internet or your church. Write down in a notebook the specific things that God impresses upon your mind. Tell someone about what you found.

2. Meditate on the Bible: Meditation simply means to regularly think about something. It is a deliberate act of the mind. An easy way to meditate is to mark verses in your Bible that God shows you in your reading and then memorize them. Look for specific applications to your life and obey God regarding the principle.

3. Pray every day: In a journal, write down your requests to God and His answers. His faithfulness will greatly encourage you. Keep a balance between requests and praise by using the ACT formula. *A* stands for adoring God for His person and greatness. *C* stands for confessing your sins and failures. *T* stands for thanking Him for what He has done and will do.

(Based on *Basics for Believers*, James A. Berg, BJUP, 1978, pp. 18, 19.)

---

Judas and a band from the religious leaders then entered the garden and approached Jesus. Judas identified Jesus with a kiss of greeting. The mob then arrested Christ. Peter took a sword and cut off the ear of one of the servants (Mark 14:47; John 18:10). We can only speculate about Peter's motivation. What could one person do against a mob? How did he manage to cut off the servant's ear? Did he raise the sword over the man's head and wildly swing it down toward his body? A trained soldier would use horizontal thrusts to disable an enemy. Foolish zeal seems to have seized the disobedient Peter.

Moses likewise acted with foolish zeal in killing the Egyptian. See Exodus 2:12.

The mob led Jesus away to an illegal trial before the Sanhedrin. Peter followed far behind and tried to blend into the crowd of servants near the inquiry (Mark 14:54). He evidently wanted to see what would happen. On two occasions a small girl identified Peter as a follower of Christ. Peter denied it both times. Finally one of the servants accused Peter of being a follower of Christ, and this time he supplemented his denial with cursing and swearing. When the rooster crowed for a second time, Peter remembered the words of Christ. Peter cried bitterly over his failures (Mark 14:72).

### PRINCIPLES APPLIED

### Peter's Epistles

The Gospel of John gives an extended account of Christ's dealing with and restoring Peter after the resurrection. Peter went on to preach mighty sermons, to witness to the Jewish nation, and to write two letters about his faith in Christ. The letters show us that Christ's life and work forever shaped and molded Peter's thoughts. Look up the following verses in Peter's Epistles, determine the event referred to, and then find the corresponding section in Mark. Remember that a true disciple of Christ will know and concentrate upon the words and deeds of his Master.

**I Peter 1:3** _____

**I Peter 1:11** _____

_____

**I Peter 1:18, 19** _____

_____

**I Peter 2:6-8** _____

**I Peter 2:22-25** _____

_____

**II Peter 1:16-21** _____

A cursory reading of the four accounts of Christ's trial may at first be confusing. None of the four presents every event. This seems to point to the confusion generated by the leadership's zeal to condemn Jesus and by the consequent rapid sequence of the events. Christ first faced a trial by the Jewish authorities. The second trial was before the Roman governor, Pontius Pilate.

Hiebert notes that the trial before the religious leaders consisted of three distinct phases. Annas, the high priest, questioned Christ, according to John 18:12-14, 19-24. Next, Christ appeared before a night session of the Sanhedrin in Matthew 26:57-65 and Mark 14:53-65. Finally, the Sanhedrin condemned Christ in the early morning in Matthew 27:1; Mark 15:1; and Luke 22:66-71 (Hiebert, 427).

### Answers

**I Peter 1:3** Resurrection, Mark 16

**I Peter 1:11** Prophets predict the suffering of Christ, Mark 14:27 and other passages

**I Peter 1:18, 19** Salvation by the blood of Christ and not by traditions, Mark 7:1-13; 14:24

**I Peter 2:6-8** Stone of offence, Mark 12:1-12

**I Peter 2:22-25** Suffering of Christ, Mark 14:53-65; 15:1-38

**II Peter 1:16-21** Transfiguration, Mark 9:2-13

The high priest and Sanhedrin delivered Jesus to Pontius Pilate for crucifixion. For six hours the Messiah hung on a cross in sheer agony. He died as the Jews mocked Him. Mark does not tell us the location of the eleven disciples during this time. They probably hid themselves, fearing that they too would be crucified. Did they agonize over the loss of their master? Did they cry over their own failures? Did they mourn the loss of a high position in the kingdom? All are likely true.

Jesus had told the disciples repeatedly that He would rise from the dead on the third day following His death. Two women went to the tomb to prepare His body for burial, and an angel greeted them. He announced Christ's Resurrection! The women were to go and "tell his disciples and **Peter** that he goeth before you to Galilee: there shall ye see him, as he said unto you [emphasis added]" (Mark 16:7). Jesus appeared to at least three other individuals who told the news to the disciples. The eleven did not believe that Jesus was alive. Finally, Jesus appeared to them and

Most conservative Bible scholars believe that Mark's Gospel is Peter's account of Christ's life. Mark's references to Peter provide us with some insight into how Peter viewed himself. In many instances, Peter's behavior is not good. He is either rebuking Christ or denying any relationship with Him. Note too that Mark says very little about Peter's restoration to Christ while John gives a detailed account of it. Perhaps we can conclude that Peter was ashamed and repentant over his actions and that those events remained fresh in his memory. From the book of Acts and from Peter's Epistles, we know that he led the church in Jerusalem and that he had a great ministry in other parts of the world. Great men of God recognize their failures, and those failures always compel them to seek Christ and His service.

## Exercise: Hymn Search

**Goal:** To consider the death of Christ through hymns.

**Procedure:** Obtain a hymnbook for each student. Allot ten minutes for each student to find ten hymns about the events in the Passion Week. Then allot ten more minutes for the students to find the hymn's basis in the gospel accounts. Write the verses down with the hymn names. Ask several to share their favorite hymns.

## Exercise: Peter's Restoration

**Goal:** To learn the details of Peter's restoration to Christ.

**Procedure:** Instruct the students to read John 21 and then to write a one-page paper on Christ's compassion in the restoration of Peter. Include why Christ would have been justified in condemning Peter, why He dealt with Peter the way He did in John 21, and what the results were later in Peter's life.

strongly rebuked their unresponsive hearts (Mark 16:14). He told them to go into the entire world and tell people about His great salvation for man's sins. Notice that even though the disciples miserably failed Jesus at the trial and crucifixion, He sought them and forgave them. Over the next years, the disciples preached to the entire known world, and scores were saved. The disciples' actions proved the reality of Christ's compassion in their own lives. The rest of their lives would now be spent telling others about Jesus Christ's love for sinners.

## Knowing Christ

The Gospel of Mark starts by proclaiming that Jesus Christ is the Son of God. His deity forms the backbone of the book. We have examined Christ's relationship to various groups of people. As both God and man, Jesus healed the sick, cast out unclean spirits, calmed the sea, rebuked religious leaders, trained His disciples, and died for sinners. Through these events, the Lord wants us to know and to understand His Son. The crucifixion of Christ forced the disciples to see themselves as weak and sinful. His Resurrection and compassion forced the disciples to transfer the facts about Christ from their heads into their hearts. Christianity is not a philosophy or a religion. It is a relationship between a believer and the Son of God. That relationship transformed Peter's cowardly denials of his Lord into bold proclamations of God's grace both in Jerusalem and around the Roman world. Peter and the disciples saw Jesus Christ in person. Mark wrote his Gospel for our benefit that we too might see Jesus. The key to a full life in this world and to eternal life in heaven is "that I may know him."

---

### Exercise: Word Search

**Goal:** To review people in Mark.

**Procedure:** Duplicate and distribute the word search in the Appendix (pp. 163-64). Allow the students to use their Bibles to look up the verses. Grade as an extra credit project.

# Review Questions

1. What Old Testament men appeared with Christ at the transfiguration?

   **Moses and Elijah**

2. Whose ministry did Jesus equate with John the Baptist's?

   **Elijah**

3. Who betrayed Jesus to the mob?

   **Judas Iscariot**

4. Who would be the greatest in the kingdom according to Jesus?

   **The servant**

5. The word *offend* means what?

   **To cause to sin**

6. How did Jesus arrive in Jerusalem?

   **Riding on a donkey or colt**

7. What did Jesus curse as a lesson on faith for the disciples?

   **Fig tree**

8. The Lord's Supper is closely associated with what Jewish observance?

   **Passover**

9. Where was Jesus betrayed?

   **The garden of Gethsemane**

10. Who told the two women about Christ's resurrection?

   *A young man in shining garments or an angel*

Write one or two complete sentences to answer the following questions.

11. Why was Jesus transfigured?

   *Jesus was transfigured to prove His deity to the three disciples and to give authority to His statements about dying.*

12. How do we know that Jesus' death was not an accident?

   *Jesus predicted His death in great detail. God the Father approved Jesus' statements about His death. Jesus purposely led the disciples to Jerusalem where He was crucified.*

13. What is the symbolic significance of salt in Mark 9?

*Salt was used as a preservative and as part of sacrifices. It symbolizes a believer's effectiveness in the world.*

14. What is the significance of the bread and wine at the Lord's Supper?

*The bread points to Christ's body while the wine points to His blood. The blood ratified the New Testament or New Covenant with believers.*

15. Why did Peter weep when the rooster crowed the second time?

*Peter wept because he had failed to publicly speak for Christ. Jesus predicted Peter's failure. Peter did not listen to Jesus. His tears proved the truthfulness of Christ's words and the weakness of Peter's convictions.*

## Photograph Credits

The following agencies and individuals have furnished materials to meet the photographic needs of this textbook. We wish to express our gratitude to them for their important contribution.

1999-2001 www.arttoday.com
American Tract Society www.ATStracts.org
Bob Jones University Collection
Christian History Institute
Mike James
Overseas Missionary Fellowship

# CONTENTS OF THE APPENDIX

# Class Reading Ideas

The most important part of this course is learning the actual text of Mark's Gospel. Lectures, group activities, overheads, worksheets, and other teaching aids must all focus on the words of Scripture. The suggested lesson plans for each chapter contain one day for reading Mark in class. You may also want to assign a reading of Mark one or more times as homework. If some part of the curriculum must be omitted, do not omit the reading. The following ideas and methods will give variety to the class reading and may motivate students to learn.

**Individual silent reading**   At least one day in the course should be dedicated to silent reading. Most devotional reading is silent, therefore the students should be encouraged to develop the skill for and an enjoyment of reading. Set a goal for the day. Those who do not finish can complete the assignment as homework.

**Teacher reading**   Read aloud while the students follow along in their Bibles. Using good vocal technique will add interest and help keep the students focused.

**Student reading**   Assign each student a chapter to read out loud to the class during the course. Encourage practice and good speaking technique.

**Pastor reading**   Invite your pastor or another spiritual leader to read to the class. This reinforces to the students the importance of reading the Scriptures.

**Audiotapes**   Obtain an audiotape of Mark and play it for the class. The students should follow along in their Bibles.

**Dramatized audiotapes**   Obtain a dramatized audiotape of Mark and play it for the class. Ask the class to evaluate the appropriateness and realism of the sound effects.

**Reading with a topical worksheet**   Choose a common topic in Mark and have the students look for that topic as they read. The students should write down the verse references as they find the topic. Topics may include faith, fear, the deity of Christ, great statements, miracles, occupations, and so forth.

**Reading an alternate translation**   Choose a different translation than is normally used in your class and school. The administrator may need to approve the choice. Avoid using a paraphrase. Following the reading, ask the students what they liked and disliked about the translation.

**Foreign language reading**   Allow the students studying a foreign language to read the same chapter to the class in the other language. The other students should follow along in their English Bibles.

**Choral reading**   Divide the class into several groups and assign one or more chapters to each group for a choral reading project. See the Internet or a speech book for specific suggestions. Allow the group to present its work to the class, to the school chapel, or to other classes. Consider video- or audio-taping the sessions.

**Skits or plays**   Divide the class into several groups and assign a specific incident in Mark to each. Have the group develop a play using as many of the actual words of Scripture as possible. Using props, costumes, and other staging techniques will add much to the exercise.

# THE POINT IS . . .

## For whatever a man's actions are, such must be his spirit.

Demosthenes (384-322 B.C.): The greatest of the Greek orators

## The actions of men are the best interpreters of their thoughts.

John Locke (1632-1704): Advocate of political and religious freedom

## Words without actions are the assassins of idealism.

Herbert Hoover (1874-1964): Thirty-first president of the United States

## I never worry about action, only inaction.

Sir Winston Churchill (1874-1965):
Prime minister of Great Britain during World War II

# THE STRUCTURE OF THE NEW TESTAMENT

## Name
"New Testament"—from the Greek word *diatheke,* "covenant"
through the Latin *testamentum,* "a will"

## Authors
8 or 9 individuals

## Size
27 books

## Time
About 50 years (latter half of the first century)

## Language
Greek

## BOOK DIVISIONS

### Histories
Gospels
Acts

### Letters
Paul's
General

### Prophecy
Revelation

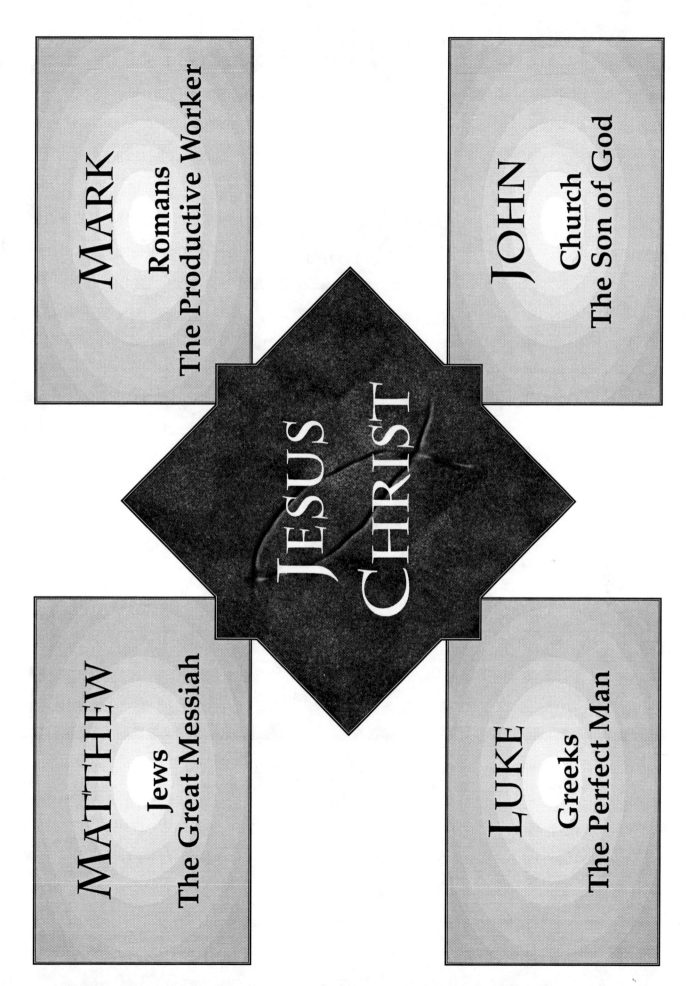

# CHRIST'S OLD TESTAMENT FOUNDATIONS

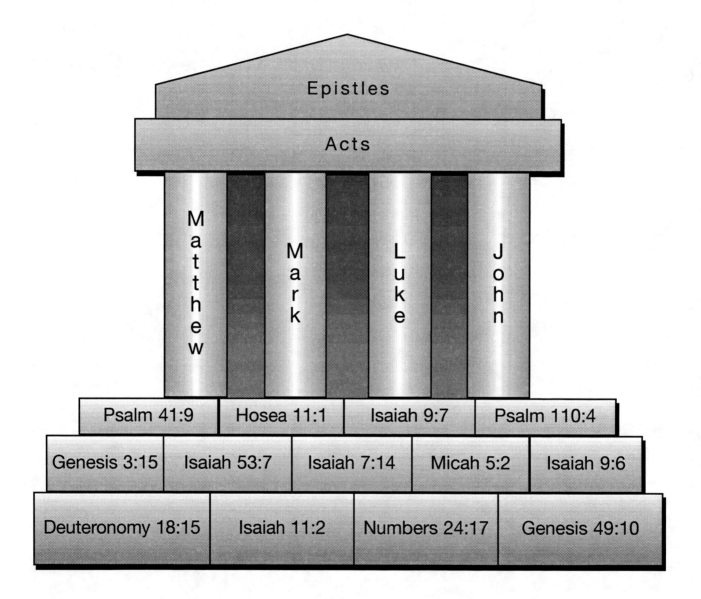

**Name** _____

# THE NAMES OF CHRIST

**Directions: Look up the verses and fill out the chart accordingly.**

| Verse | Name of Christ | Who used the name? |
|---|---|---|
| Mark 4:38 | | |
| Mark 6:3 | | |
| Mark 6:15 | | |
| Mark 10:48 | | |
| Mark 15:2 | | |
| Mark 15:32 | | |
| Mark 1:24 | | |
| Mark 1:24 | | |
| Mark 14:27 | | |
| Mark 15:39 | | |
| Mark 5:7 | | |
| Mark 1:11 | | |

**Find at least five verses in which Jesus is called the "Son of man."**

## NAMES HAVE SIGNIFICANCE IN THE BIBLE!

# THE NAMES OF CHRIST

**Directions: Look up the verses and fill out the chart accordingly.**

| Verse | Name of Christ | Who used the name? |
|---|---|---|
| Mark 4:38 | Master | Disciples |
| Mark 6:3 | The carpenter | People of Nazareth |
| Mark 6:15 | Prophet | People |
| Mark 10:48 | Son of David | Bartimaeus |
| Mark 15:2 | King of the Jews | Pilate |
| Mark 15:32 | King of Israel | Chief Priests |
| Mark 1:24 | Jesus of Nazareth | Unclean spirit |
| Mark 1:24 | Holy One of God | Unclean spirit |
| Mark 14:27 | Shepherd | Jesus |
| Mark 15:39 | Son of God | Centurion |
| Mark 5:7 | Son of the Most High God | Legion (Unclean spirits) |
| Mark 1:11 | My beloved Son | God |

**Find at least five verses in which Jesus is called the "Son of man."**

| | | | | |
|---|---|---|---|---|
| 2:10 | 8:38 | 9:31 | 13:26 | 14:41 |
| 2:28 | 9:9 | 10:33 | 13:34 | 14:62 |
| 8:31 | 9:12 | 10:45 | 14:21 | |

## NAMES HAVE SIGNIFICANCE IN THE BIBLE!

# TEACHINGS OF CHRIST IN MARK

## He that hath ears to hear let him hear!

**Jesus taught constantly while on earth. Learning to analyze His teachings will help us to apply them to our lives. Read each passage in Mark. State the basic theme of the lesson in one short sentence.**

| Verses | Teacher | Students | Lessons |
|--------|---------|----------|---------|
| 1:14, 15 | Jesus | People of Galilee | Repent and believe in order to enter the kingdom. |
| 6:7-11 | | | |
| 6:45-52 | | | |
| 9:30-32 | | | |
| 10:13-16 | | | |
| 10:23-27 | | | |
| 13:1-37 | | | |

# TEACHINGS OF CHRIST IN MARK

He that hath ears to hear let him hear!

**Jesus taught constantly while on earth. Learning to analyze His teachings will help us to apply them to our lives. Read each passage in Mark. State the basic theme of the lesson in one short sentence.**

| Verses | Teacher | Students | Lessons |
|---|---|---|---|
| 1:14, 15 | Jesus | People of Galilee | Repent and believe in order to enter the kingdom. |
| 6:7-11 | Jesus | Disciples | Jesus tells the disciples how to work in the kingdom of God. |
| 6:45-52 | Jesus | Disciples | Jesus can protect His people by His presence and calm the fears of His people. |
| 9:30-32 | Jesus | Disciples | Jesus would be killed. |
| 10:13-16 | Jesus | Disciples, others | People must enter the kingdom as small children. |
| 10:23-27 | Jesus | Disciples | Riches prevent many people from entering the kingdom. |
| 13:1-37 | Jesus | Peter, James, John, Andrew | Jesus knows and controls the future. |

# ROMAN DOMINATION OF PALESTINE

| Pompey |
| --- |
| (Roman General) |
| Conquered Palestine 63 B.C. |

↓

| Antipater |
| --- |
| (Procurator of Judea 47-43 B.C.) |
| Appointed by Julius Caesar |

↓

| Herod |
| --- |
| (King of Judea 37-4 B.C.) |
| Appointed by Augustus |

sons of Herod

| Archelaus | Herod Antipas | Philip the Tetrarch |
| --- | --- | --- |
| Judea, Samaria, Idumea | Galilee, Perea | Batanea, Trachonitis, Auranitis |
| 4 B.C.-A.D. 6 | 4 B.C.-A.D. 39 | 4 B.C.-A.D. 34 |
| Banished by Roman government for incompetence | Built city of Tiberias Killed John the Baptist | Built Caesarea Philippi |

↓

| Valerius Gratus |
| --- |
| (Roman Procurator) |
| Judea, Samaria, Idumea |
| A.D. 15-26 |

↓

| Pontius Pilate |
| --- |
| (Roman Procurator) |
| Judea, Samaria, Idumea |
| A.D. 26-36 |

Name —————————

# LEPROSY IN THE BIBLE

**Directions: Look up each passage and fill out the blank spaces with the appropriate information.**

| Passage | Person or People | Cause | Lessons |
|---|---|---|---|
| Numbers 5:1-4 | | | |
| Numbers 12 | | | |
| Deuteronomy 24:8 | | | |
| II Kings 5:1-19 | | | |
| II Kings 5:20-27 | | | |
| II Kings 7 | | | |
| II Kings 15:1-7 | | | |
| Luke 17:11-19 | | | |

# LEPROSY IN THE BIBLE

**Directions: Look up each passage and fill out the blank spaces with the appropriate information.**

| Passage | Person or People | Cause | Lessons |
|---|---|---|---|
| Numbers 5:1-4 | Lepers in the camp | not specified | Leprosy causes defilement and leads to separation from others. |
| Numbers 12 | Miriam | God's judgment | Leprosy may be a judgment of God against the sin of rebellion. Leprosy is associated with death. Leprosy may be healed. |
| Deuteronomy 24:8 | Israel | not specified | Be obedient to God's commands when dealing with leprosy. |
| II Kings 5:1-19 | Naaman | not specified | God specifies the methods of healing for leprosy. God is able to heal. |
| II Kings 5:20-27 | Gehazi | God's judgment | God's judgment for sin is very serious. |
| II Kings 7 | Four lepers | not specified | Leprosy causes separation from others. God may use lepers to proclaim His works. |
| II Kings 15:1-7 | Azariah | God's judgment | God's judgment for incomplete obedience is very serious. |
| Luke 17:11-19 | Ten lepers | not specified | Christ can heal leprosy. People are not thankful for God's goodness in their lives. Faith is critical to a relationship with God. |

# REPORTERS IN ACTION

**Directions: Journalists often ask people a series of questions in order to understand a situation. As a newspaper reporter, read the assigned passage in Mark and find the answers to the following questions. Write a one-sentence headline that could grab the attention of a reader.**

Passage: _____

1. Who? (List all the people and then decide who the main character is.)

2. What? (Describe the specific facts of the situation.)

3. Where? (Where do the events occur? Is there any significance to the location?)

4. When? (When do the events occur? Is there any important sequence of events?)

5. How? (How do the events occur? What motivates the main characters in the events?)

6. Why? (Why are these events recorded in the Bible?)

**Headline:**

# IDENTIFYING THE FORCES OF EVIL

# Names

**Satan**—adversary: Matthew 4:10

**Devil**—slanderer, accuser: Matthew 4:1

**Apollyon**—destroyer: Revelation 9:11

**Beelzebub**—lord of the dwelling: Mark 3:22

# Descriptions

**Demons**—hostile to God; Matthew 8:29

**Prince of Devils**—Matthew 12:24

**Prince of the Power of the Air**—Ephesians 2:2

**Prince of This World**—John 14:30

**God of This World**—II Corinthians 4:4

**Murderer**—John 8:44

**Accuser of Our Brethren**—Revelation 12:10

**Ruler of Darkness**—Ephesians 6:12

# CHRIST'S TRANSFORMING POWER

Christ completely changed the life of the man in Mark 5:1-20. He wants to change us as well.

**Read the passage and then fill out the chart with a brief description of the situation and the verse reference. On the back, write a paragraph on how Christ changed your life when you trusted Him. Ask your teacher or parents about other areas you need to change.**

| Question | Before | After |
|---|---|---|
| Where did the man live? | | |
| Who influenced the man? | | |
| How did he behave? | | |
| What was the man normally doing? | | |

# CHRIST'S TRANSFORMING POWER

Christ completely changed the life of the man in Mark 5:1-20. He wants to change us as well.

**Read the passage and then fill out the chart with a brief description of the situation and the verse reference. On the back, write a paragraph on how Christ changed your life when you trusted Him. Ask your teacher or parents about other areas you need to change.**

| Question | Before | After |
|---|---|---|
| Where did the man live? | Tombs, vv. 2, 3 | With people, vv. 19, 20 |
| Who influenced the man? | Unclean spirit, v. 2 | Christ, vv. 8, 19 |
| How did he behave? | Untameable, uncontrollable, and threatening, vv. 3, 4 | Normally: sitting, clothed, in right mind, v. 15 |
| What was the man normally doing? | Crying and cutting himself; being destructive, v. 5 | Learning from Christ, vv. 15, 18, 19, witnessing for Christ, v. 20 |

# THE BATTLEFIELDS

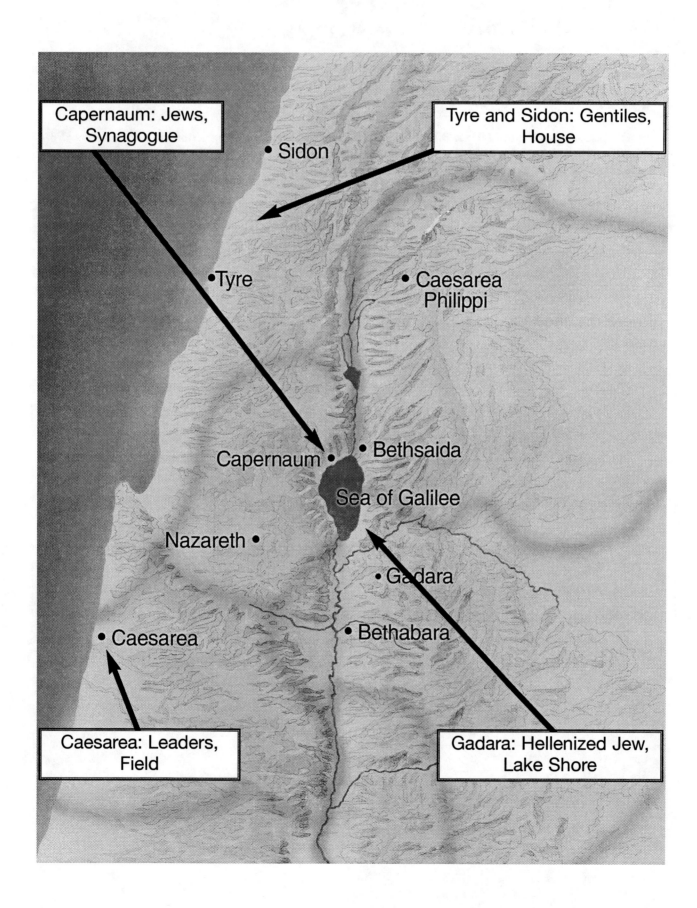

Capernaum: Jews, Synagogue

Tyre and Sidon: Gentiles, House

• Sidon

•Tyre

• Caesarea Philippi

Capernaum •

• Bethsaida

Sea of Galilee

Nazareth •

• Gadara

• Caesarea

• Bethabara

Caesarea: Leaders, Field

Gadara: Hellenized Jew, Lake Shore

© 2002 BJU Press. Limited license to copy granted on copyright page.

# CHRIST DEALS WITH THE RELIGIOUS LEADERSHIP

**Directions: Look up each passage in Mark and fill out the chart accordingly. Summarize the main issue in a phrase or short sentence.**

| Verses | Religious Group(s) | Location | Issue |
|---|---|---|---|
| 2:1-12 | | | |
| 2:13-17 | | | |
| 2:18-22 | | | |
| 2:23-28 | | | |
| 3:1-6 | | | |
| 3:22-30 | | | |
| 5:21-43 | | | |
| 7:1-23 | | | |
| 8:10-13 | | | |
| 8:14-21 | | | |
| 9:14-29 | | | |
| 10:1-12 | | | |
| 10:32-34 | | | |
| 11:15-19 | | | |
| 11:27-33 | | | |

# CHRIST DEALS WITH THE RELIGIOUS LEADERSHIP (CONT.)

| | | | |
|---|---|---|---|
| 12:1-12 | | | |
| 12:13-17 | | | |
| 12:18-27 | | | |
| 12:28-34 | | | |
| 12:35-37 | | | |
| 12:38-40 | | | |
| 14:41-72 | | | |
| 15:1-47 | | | |

# CHRIST DEALS WITH THE RELIGIOUS LEADERSHIP

**Directions: Look up each passage in Mark and fill out the chart accordingly. Summarize the main issue in a phrase or short sentence.**

| Verses | Religious Group(s) | Location | Issue |
|---|---|---|---|
| 2:1-12 | Scribes | Capernaum | Jesus forgives sins. |
| 2:13-17 | Scribes and Pharisees | Capernaum | Jesus eats with sinners. |
| 2:18-22 | Disciples of John and disciples of the Pharisees | Capernaum | Jesus' disciples do not fast. |
| 2:23-28 | Pharisees | Capernaum | Jesus' disciples pick grain on the Sabbath. |
| 3:1-6 | Pharisees, Herodians | Capernaum | Jesus heals on the Sabbath. |
| 3:22-30 | Scribes | Galilee | Jesus reveals His source of power. |
| 5:21-43 | Jairus, ruler of a synagogue | Galilee | Jesus heals a girl due to her father's faith. |
| 7:1-23 | Scribes and Pharisees | Galilee | Jesus teaches about traditions. |
| 8:10-13 | Pharisees | Galilee (Dalmanutha) | Jesus refuses to give a sign. |
| 8:14-21 | Pharisees | Galilee | Jesus teaches about false doctrine. |
| 9:14-29 | Scribes | Caesarea Philippi | Jesus rebukes the scribes and disciples. |
| 10:1-12 | Pharisees | Jordan | Jesus teaches about divorce. |
| 10:32-34 | Chief priests, scribes | Jerusalem | Jesus foretells His death to the disciples. |
| 11:15-19 | Chief priests, scribes | Jerusalem | Jesus removes the moneychangers. |
| 11:27-33 | Chief priests, scribes, elders | Jerusalem | Jesus rebukes the leaders for unbelief. |

# CHRIST DEALS WITH THE RELIGIOUS LEADERSHIP (CONT.)

| 12:1-12 | Leaders | Jerusalem | Jesus teaches by parables about rejection of Him. |
|---|---|---|---|
| 12:13-17 | Pharisees, Herodians | Jerusalem | Jesus teaches about taxes. |
| 12:18-27 | Sadducees | Jerusalem | Jesus teaches about resurrection. |
| 12:28-34 | A scribe | Jerusalem | Jesus teaches about the greatest commandment. |
| 12:35-37 | Scribes | Jerusalem | Jesus teaches about the Messiah. |
| 12:38-40 | Scribes | Jerusalem | Jesus warns against religion that is merely external. |
| 14:41-72 | Leaders | Jerusalem | Jesus is arrested and put on trial. |
| 15:1-47 | Leaders | Jerusalem | Jesus is crucified. |

# CHRIST VERSUS RELIGION

**Directions: Look up each passage and fill out the blank spaces with the appropriate information.**

| Verses | Christ | Religion |
|---|---|---|
| 2:1-12 | | |
| 2:13-17 | | |
| 2:18-22 | | |
| 2:23–3:6 | | |
| 3:22-30 | | |
| 7:1-13 | | |
| 7:14-23 | | |
| 11:15-19 | | |
| 12:41-37 | | |
| 14:1-72 | | |

## CHRIST VERSUS RELIGION

**Directions: Look up each passage and fill out the blank spaces with the appropriate information.**

| Verses | Christ | Religion |
|---|---|---|
| 2:1-12 | Cares for the sick<br>Forgives sins | Does not recognize the true person of Christ |
| 2:13-17 | Calls sinners to repentance | Avoids man's main problem of sin |
| 2:18-22 | Offers abundant life | Adheres to marginal practices |
| 2:23–3:6 | Puts compassion above tradition | Adheres to worthless traditions |
| 3:22-30 | Works in the power of the Spirit | Slanders the evidences of Christ's power |
| 7:1-13 | Exposes wicked and false practices | Substitutes tradition for Scripture |
| 7:14-23 | Points to man's internal wickedness | Claims man has internal goodness |
| 11:15-19 | Removes corruption from holy places | Seeks financial gain from religion |
| 12:18-37 | Answers difficult questions with Scripture | Fails to answer difficult questions by religious system |
| 14:1-72 | Testifies to the truth | Rejects the truth |

# CROSSWORD PUZZLE: PEOPLE AND EVENTS IN MARK

## DOWN

1. The sixth-listed disciple of Jesus
2. Jesus quotes his Psalm 110 in chapter 12.
3. A disciple whose other name was Simon
4. The son of Timaeus who was healed
5. Young man who turned from Jesus when he was told to sell his belongings
6. Jesus was first brought before this official after His arrest (ch. 14).
8. Begged Christ to heal her daughter (ch. 7)
11. Peter's brother
12. A Cyrenian; carried Jesus' cross
14. A son of thunder
17. Came to anoint Christ's body
18. Released instead of Jesus
20. Man who had an impediment of speech; healed by Jesus (ch. 7)
21. OT prophet quoted to the Pharisees by Jesus (ch. 7)

22. This John was the forerunner of Christ.
23. The Gospel of Mark was written about this man.

## ACROSS

1. A man who was this was healed in chapter 8.
3. Another disciple
7. A man of this people had an evil spirit cast out by Jesus (ch. 5).
9. Sat at the receipt of customs; a disciple
10. Simon was this (14:3).
12. Tempted Jesus in the wilderness
13. Listed before Simon the Canaanite (ch. 3)
15. A disciple of Christ
16. Had an issue of blood (ch. 5)
19. Christ's betrayer
24. A woman with this type of box anointed Jesus' head (ch. 14).
25. Led Jesus into the wilderness (ch. 1)

# CROSSWORD PUZZLE: PEOPLE AND EVENTS IN MARK

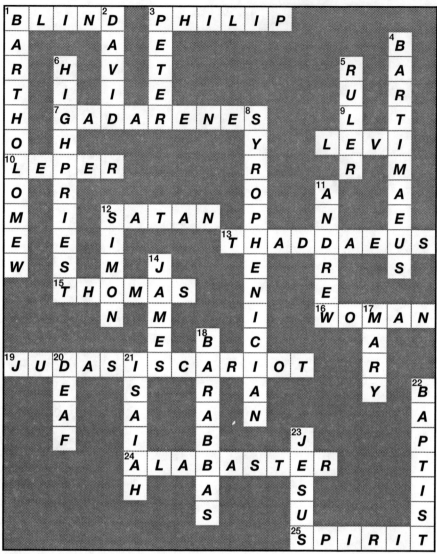

**DOWN**

1. The sixth-listed disciple of Jesus
2. Jesus quotes his Psalm 110 in chapter 12.
3. A disciple whose other name was Simon
4. The son of Timaeus who was healed
5. Young man who turned from Jesus when he was told to sell his belongings
6. Jesus was first brought before this official after His arrest (ch. 14).
8. Begged Christ to heal her daughter (ch. 7)
11. Peter's brother
12. A Cyrenian; carried Jesus' cross
14. A son of thunder
17. Came to anoint Christ's body
18. Released instead of Jesus
20. Man who had an impediment of speech; healed by Jesus (ch. 7)
21. OT prophet quoted to the Pharisees by Jesus (ch. 7)

22. This John was the forerunner of Christ.
23. The Gospel of Mark was written about this man.

**ACROSS**

1. A man who was this was healed in chapter 8.
3. Another disciple
7. A man of this people had an evil spirit cast out by Jesus (ch. 5).
9. Sat at the receipt of customs; a disciple
10. Simon was this (14:3).
12. Tempted Jesus in the wilderness
13. Listed before Simon the Canaanite (ch. 3)
15. A disciple of Christ
16. Had an issue of blood (ch. 5)
19. Christ's betrayer
24. A woman with this type of box anointed Jesus' head (ch. 14).
25. Led Jesus into the wilderness (ch. 1)

Name _____

# GREAT STATEMENTS IN MARK

**Look up the verses and fill out the chart accordingly. Construct a one-sentence personal application for each verse.**

| Verses | Speaker | Audience | Statement | Application to Me |
|---|---|---|---|---|
| 1:1 | Mark | Readers | The beginning of the gospel of Jesus Christ, the Son of God. | Mark is about the deity of Christ. |
| 2:5 | | | | |
| 3:11 | | | | |
| 4:39 | | | | |
| 5:36 | | | | |
| 6:50 | | | | |
| 7:28 | | | | |

**Name**

# GREAT STATEMENTS IN MARK (CONT.)

| | | | |
|---|---|---|---|
| 8:27 | | | |
| 9:6 | | | |
| 10:52 | | | |
| 11:10 | | | |
| 12:24 | | | |
| 13:37 | | | |
| 14:24 | | | |
| 15:34 | | | |
| 16:15 | | | |

Name _____

# Great Statements in Mark

**Look up the verses and fill out the chart accordingly. Construct a one-sentence personal application for each verse.**

| Verses | Speaker | Audience | Statement | Application to Me |
|--------|---------|----------|-----------|-------------------|
| 1:1 | Mark | Readers | The beginning of the gospel of Jesus Christ, the Son of God. | Mark is about the deity of Christ. |
| 2:5 | Christ | Palsied man | Son, thy sins be forgiven thee. | Jesus can forgive our sins. |
| 3:11 | Unclean spirits | Christ | Thou art the Son of God. | Even the devil's confederates recognize Christ. So should I. |
| 4:39 | Christ | Weather, disciples | Peace, be still. | Christ controls nature. |
| 5:36 | Christ | Jairus | Be not afraid, only believe. | I must believe Christ. |
| 6:50 | Christ | Disciples | Be of good cheer: it is I; be not afraid. | Fear departs in the presence of Christ. |
| 7:28 | Woman | Christ | Yes, Lord: yet the dogs under the table eat of the children's crumbs. | Christ's grace is sufficient for all. |

# GREAT STATEMENTS IN MARK (CONT.)

ANSWER KEY

| | | | |
|---|---|---|---|
| 8:27 | Christ | Disciples | Whom do men say that I am? | I must recognize Christ. |
| 9:7 | God | Three disciples | This is my beloved Son: hear him. | I must listen to Christ. |
| 10:52 | Christ | Bartimaeus | Go thy way; thy faith hath made thee whole. | I must believe. |
| 11:10 | Crowds | Christ | Hosanna in the highest! | I must praise the Lord. |
| 12:24 | Christ | Sadducees | Do ye not therefore err, because ye know not the scriptures, neither the power of God? | I must know the Scriptures. |
| 13:37 | Christ | Disciples | And what I say unto you I say unto all, Watch. | I must be watchful about spiritual matters. |
| 14:24 | Christ | Disciples | This is my blood of the new testament, which is shed for many. | I have salvation through the blood of Christ. |
| 15:34 | Christ | God | My God, my God, why hast thou forsaken me? | Christ's suffering is the basis of my salvation. |
| 16:15 | Christ | Disciples | Go ye into all the world, and preach the gospel to every creature. | I have a job to do. |

162

Name _____

# WORD SEARCH: PEOPLE IN MARK

**Look up the following verses to find important people in Mark. Find and circle the names in the word search below.**

```
J  E  S  Y  R  O  P  H  E  N  I  C  I  A  N  R  J  T  I  K
A  A  C  H  A  R  I  L  J  E  S  A  S  Y  R  O  O  A  S  M
H  Y  M  N  C  D  L  G  O  F  L  E  K  O  N  I  S  R  U  T
R  E  B  E  K  M  A  S  H  B  E  S  I  U  R  L  E  A  N  M
L  A  K  E  S  A  T  A  N  R  V  E  E  A  S  O  P  A  I  S
H  E  R  O  D  L  E  O  T  S  I  K  C  N  E  V  H  I  N  I
E  G  A  R  N  E  T  T  H  A  B  S  B  D  Y  A  O  L  S  M
N  O  M  S  A  D  E  T  E  H  I  I  S  R  P  U  F  Z  Z  O
E  L  E  A  U  N  H  O  B  S  O  N  J  E  M  Y  A  T  R  N
L  M  N  B  A  R  T  I  A  L  B  Y  S  W  F  S  R  T  C  T
A  H  W  B  R  Z  B  D  P  E  T  E  R  S  T  N  I  X  T  H
D  R  M  A  G  R  U  Y  T  H  O  L  Y  S  P  R  M  A  C  E
G  I  A  R  M  J  N  O  I  B  E  T  T  E  I  R  A  O  F  L
A  T  H  A  A  N  I  W  S  A  S  F  O  P  U  R  T  M  I  E
M  N  U  B  T  E  S  A  T  G  O  B  S  E  C  A  H  U  S  P
Y  I  M  O  S  E  S  D  I  D  N  Y  O  T  F  I  E  N  D  E
R  A  S  U  R  I  A  J  N  Y  L  T  H  I  N  G  A  D  I  R
A  F  F  E  N  T  O  H  W  O  E  L  L  V  O  L  U  M  E  T
M  T  R  J  O  H  N  I  H  T  S  I  R  H  C  S  U  S  E  J
```

## The Words:

| | | |
|---|---|---|
| 1:1 | 5:22 | 14:33 (3 people) |
| 1:4 | 6:14 | 15:7 |
| 1:13 | 7:10 | 15:14 |
| 2:14 | 7:26 | 15:43 |
| 4:10 | 14:3 | 16:9 |

# WORD SEARCH: PEOPLE IN MARK

**Look up the following verses to find important people in Mark. Find and circle the names in the word search below.**

```
J E S Y R O P H E N I C I A N R J T I K
A A C H A R I L J E S A S Y R O O A S M
H Y M N C D L G O F L E K O N I S R U T
R E B E K M A S H B E S I U R L E A N M
L A K E S A T A N R V E E A S O P A I S
H E R O D L E O T S I K C N E V H I N I
E G A R N E T T H A B S B D Y A O L S M
N O M S A D E T E H I I S R P U F Z Z O
E L E A U N H O B S O N J E M Y A T R N
L M N B A R T I A L B Y S W F S R T C T
A H W B R Z B D P E T E R S T N I X T H
D R M A G R U Y T H O L Y S P R M A C E
G I A R M J N O I B E T T E I R A O F L
A T H A A N I W S A S F O P U R T M I E
M N U B T E S A T G O B S E C A H U S P
Y I M O S E S D I D N Y O T F I E N D E
R A S U R I A J N Y L T H I N G A D I R
A F F E N T O H W O E L L V O L U M E T
M T R J O H N I H T S I R H C S U S E J
```

**The Words:**

| | | | | | | |
|---|---|---|---|---|---|---|
| 1:1 | Jesus Christ | 5:22 | Jairus | 14:33 | Peter, James, John |
| 1:4 | John the Baptist | 6:14 | Herod | 15:7 | Barabbas |
| 1:13 | Satan | 7:10 | Moses | 15:14 | Pilate |
| 2:14 | Levi | 7:26 | Syrophenician | 15:43 | Joseph of Arimathea |
| 4:10 | Judas Iscariot | 14:3 | Simon the Leper | 16:9 | Mary Magdalene |

# Bibliography

The following works were consulted while preparing *That I May Know Him*. If at all possible, the teacher should obtain at least one good commentary to supplement the study of Mark. *That I May Know Him* is not a commentary but rather an aid to learning the text of Mark. Space limitations and the purpose of the book do not allow the coverage of many technical or interpretational issues.

Beale, David. *A Pictorial History of Our English Bible.* Greenville, SC: Bob Jones UP, 1982.

*Biblical Viewpoint* 11, no. 2 (November 1977). The theological journal of the BJU School of Religion contains articles on selected chapters and an extensive bibliography.

Cole, R. A. *The Gospel According to St. Mark.* Grand Rapids: Eerdmans, 1988. Cole summarizes key events and teachings while explaining difficult issues. I do not always agree with his conclusions but do find the book to be very helpful. 263 pp.

Edersheim, Alfred. *The Life and Times of Jesus the Messiah.* 2 vols. Grand Rapids: Eerdmans, 1977. This is a classic work from a Jewish perspective of the Gospels. The reading can be tedious due to its length and style. Many modern commentators extensively use and quote Edersheim. Every serious student of the Gospels should invest in this book. 1523 pp.

Henry, Matthew. *A Commentary on the Whole Bible,* Vol. 5. Iowa Falls, Iowa: World Bible Publishers, n. d. Matthew Henry's timeless work is a great addition to any library.

Hiebert, D. Edmond. *The Gospel of Mark.* Greenville, SC: Bob Jones University Press 1994. This is the single most useful work on Mark. Hiebert combines outstanding scholarship with genuine spiritual insight. It is also very readable even in fairly technical sections. 516 pp.

Hobbs, Herschel H. *An Exposition of the Gospel of Mark.* Grand Rapids: Baker Book House, 1970. Hobbs's work contains good conservative scholarship and a warm devotional spirit. He provides adequate summaries of each paragraph but does not examine each detail of the text. 261 pp.

*International Standard Bible Encyclopedia.* 5 vols. Grand Rapids: Eerdmans, 1978.

Lenski, R.C.H. *The Interpretation of St. Mark's Gospel.* Minneapolis: Augsburg Publishing House, 1964. Lenski writes from a Lutheran background and has many good insights into the text. 775 pp.

Swete, Henry Barclay. *Commentary on Mark.* Grand Rapids: Kregel Publications, 1977. This is an extensive work on the Greek text of Mark. Those with a good background in Greek will appreciate Swete's insights, but I do not recommend his book for those who do not read Greek. 434 pp.

*The New Bible Dictionary.* Wheaton, IL: Tyndale House Publishers, Inc., 1962.

Thiessen, Henry Clarence. *Lectures in Systematic Theology.* Grand Rapids: Eerdmans, 1949.

Trench, R. C. *Notes on the Parables of Our Lord.* Grand Rapids: Baker Book House, 1977. This is the classic work on New Testament parables. 211 pp.

## Multiple Choice

Choose the correct answer.

_____ 1. Those anointed in the Old Testament include all except

   A. kings.
   B. scribes.
   C. priests.
   D. prophets.
   E. none of the above

_____ 2. Jesus used this method to cast out unclean spirits.

   A. He spoke.
   B. He prayed.
   C. He read from the Prophets.
   D. He called for the priests.
   E. none of the above

_____ 3. This person announced Jesus' coming to the Jews.

   A. Peter
   B. Paul
   C. John the Baptist
   D. Nicodemus
   E. none of the above

_____ 4. Legion refers to

   A. a town in Galilee.
   B. Roman soldiers.
   C. an infected wound.
   D. an important Pharisee.
   E. none of the above

_____ 5. Jesus' boyhood home was in

   A. Jerusalem.
   B. Capernaum.
   C. Gadara.
   D. Nazareth.
   E. none of the above

_____ 6. Who was the "strong man" when Jesus spoke to the religious leaders about the divided house?

   A. Peter
   B. John the Baptist
   C. Satan
   D. Jesus
   E. none of the above

_____ 7. In the parable of the soils, the stony ground represented people who

   A. abandon the truth when circumstances are hard.
   B. are indifferent to the truth.
   C. respond to the truth and bear fruit.
   D. place more value on things than on the truth.
   E. all of the above

_____ 8. Which method was commonly used by rabbis to heal lepers?

　　A. The rabbi touched the leper's forehead.
　　B. The rabbi provided medicine for the leper.
　　C. The rabbi prayed over the leper.
　　D. all of the above
　　E. none of the above

## Matching

Choose the best answer from the list for each item.

　　A. God with us　　　　　　　D. Anointed One
　　B. Son of David　　　　　　E. Equal to God
　　C. Jesus' name for Himself　　F. Jehovah saves

_____ 9. Jesus

_____ 10. Christ

_____ 11. Son of man

_____ 12. Son of God

_____ 13. Emmanuel

## True/False

_____ 14. Jesus won the battle against evil in our place.

_____ 15. Eusebius is a minor character in Mark's Gospel.

_____ 16. Jesus used a traditional herbal medicine to heal Peter's mother-in-law.

_____ 17. English grammar is not an important Bible study tool.

_____ 18. Jesus spoke for God; therefore He was a prophet.

_____ 19. Fanny Crosby was blinded by a cholera epidemic.

_____ 20. *Ransom* means "payment."

_____ 21. Jesus' healing ministry pointed to the fact that He was the Messiah.

_____ 22. The Roman government lasted about five hundred years.

_____ 23. Jesus' actions confirmed that He was Israel's king.

_____ 24. It is a good idea to take someone with you when visiting in the hospital.

_____ 25. Jesus invented teaching in parables.

_____ 26. Jesus was amazed at the lack of faith of the people in His hometown synagogue.

## Matching

Choose the best answer from the list for each item.

A. *The Pilgrim's Progress*      G. Prince of Devils
B. Roman general               H. Canon
C. Historian                   I. Jewish traditions
D. Builder of Jerusalem        J. Synagogue leader
E. Ruler of Galilee            K. Law code
F. Adversary

_____ 27. Pompey

_____ 28. Bunyan

_____ 29. Talmud

_____ 30. Hammurabi

_____ 31. Beelzebub

_____ 32. Josephus

_____ 33. Herod Antipas

_____ 34. Satan

_____ 35. Jairus

## Short Answer

Write the answer in the space provided.

36. _____ was the city where John Mark lived.

37. Mark wrote _____ account of Christ's life.

38. Mark wrote in the _____ language.

39. The word *gospel* means _____.

40. Jesus traveled to the Gentile cities of _____ and _____.

*That I May Know Him*                    **Chapters 1-4**                    *Page 4*

### Essay

Write one or two complete sentences to answer each question.

41. What is the purpose of prayer and fasting? _____

_____

_____

42. What was the common Jewish concept of the kingdom? _____

_____

_____

43. Why did Jesus allow the unclean spirits to enter the swine? _____

_____

_____

_____

44. Why did Jesus leave Capernaum after healing Peter's mother-in-law? _____

_____

_____

45. Why did Jesus command the unclean spirits to be silent? _____

_____

_____

46. How can sickness result in a closer relationship to God? _____

_____

_____

47. Why did Jesus teach in parables? _____

_____

_____

_____

48. Why did Jesus command people not to talk about His healing them? _____

_____

_____

_____

49. What was the defect in the faith of the woman with an issue of blood? _____

_____

_____

_____

50. For what would a Bible student use a concordance? _____

_____

_____

_____

**Multiple Choice**

Choose the correct answer.

**B** 1. Those anointed in the Old Testament include all except

    A. kings.          D. prophets.
    B. scribes.        E. none of the above
    C. priests.

**A** 2. Jesus used this method to cast out unclean spirits.

    A. He spoke.        D. He called for the priests.
    B. He prayed.        E. none of the above
    C. He read from the Prophets.

**C** 3. This person announced Jesus' coming to the Jews.

    A. Peter        D. Nicodemus
    B. Paul        E. none of the above
    C. John the Baptist

**B** 4. Legion refers to

    A. a town in Galilee.        D. an important Pharisee.
    B. Roman soldiers.        E. none of the above
    C. an infected wound.

**D** 5. Jesus' boyhood home was in

    A. Jerusalem.        D. Nazareth.
    B. Capernaum.        E. none of the above
    C. Gadara.

**C** 6. Who was the "strong man" when Jesus spoke to the religious leaders about the divided house?

    A. Peter        D. Jesus
    B. John the Baptist        E. none of the above
    C. Satan

**A** 7. In the parable of the soils, the stony ground represented people who

    A. abandon the truth when circumstances are hard.
    B. are indifferent to the truth.
    C. respond to the truth and bear fruit.
    D. place more value on things than on the truth.
    E. all of the above

_____E_____  8.  Which method was commonly used by rabbis to heal lepers?

        A.  The rabbi touched the leper's forehead.
        B.  The rabbi provided medicine for the leper.
        C.  The rabbi prayed over the leper.
        D.  all of the above
        E.  none of the above

## Matching

Choose the best answer from the list for each item.

      A.  God with us              D.  Anointed One
      B.  Son of David            E.  Equal to God
      C.  Jesus' name for Himself     F.  Jehovah saves

_____F_____  9.  Jesus

_____D_____  10.  Christ

_____C_____  11.  Son of man

_____E_____  12.  Son of God

_____A_____  13.  Emmanuel

## True/False

_____T_____  14.  Jesus won the battle against evil in our place.

_____F_____  15.  Eusebius is a minor character in Mark's Gospel.

_____F_____  16.  Jesus used a traditional herbal medicine to heal Peter's mother-in-law.

_____F_____  17.  English grammar is not an important Bible study tool.

_____T_____  18.  Jesus spoke for God; therefore He was a prophet.

_____F_____  19.  Fanny Crosby was blinded by a cholera epidemic.

_____T_____  20.  *Ransom* means "payment."

_____T_____  21.  Jesus' healing ministry pointed to the fact that He was the Messiah.

_____F_____  22.  The Roman government lasted about five hundred years.

_____T_____  23.  Jesus' actions confirmed that He was Israel's king.

_____T_____  24.  It is a good idea to take someone with you when visiting in the hospital.

_____F_____  25.  Jesus invented teaching in parables.

_____T_____  26.  Jesus was amazed at the lack of faith of the people in His hometown synagogue.

## Matching

Choose the best answer from the list for each item.

A. *The Pilgrim's Progress*
B. Roman general
C. Historian
D. Builder of Jerusalem
E. Ruler of Galilee
F. Adversary

G. Prince of Devils
H. Canon
I. Jewish traditions
J. Synagogue leader
K. Law code

**B** 27. Pompey

**A** 28. Bunyan

**I** 29. Talmud

**K** 30. Hammurabi

**G** 31. Beelzebub

**C** 32. Josephus

**E** 33. Herod Antipas

**F** 34. Satan

**J** 35. Jairus

## Short Answer

Write the answer in the space provided.

36. _____ **Jerusalem** _____ was the city where John Mark lived.

37. Mark wrote _____ **Peter's** _____ account of Christ's life.

38. Mark wrote in the _____ **Greek** _____ language.

39. The word *gospel* means _____ **good news** _____.

40. Jesus traveled to the Gentile cities of _____ **Tyre** _____ and _____ **Sidon** _____.

**Essay**

Write one or two complete sentences to answer each question.

41. What is the purpose of prayer and fasting? _____

    *Prayer and fasting should bring us closer to God, resulting in spiritual power.*

    _____

42. What was the common Jewish concept of the kingdom? _____

    *The Jews wanted a political kingdom that would liberate them from foreign rule.*

    _____

43. Why did Jesus allow the unclean spirits to enter the swine? _____

    *Jesus allowed the unclean spirits to enter the swine so that people would know*

    *He had cast them out of the man.*

    _____

44. Why did Jesus leave Capernaum after healing Peter's mother-in-law? _____

    *Jesus did not seek a healing ministry. He came to preach the gospel.*

    _____

45. Why did Jesus command the unclean spirits to be silent? _____

    *Jesus showed His control of the unclean spirits and would not allow them*

    *to testify about Himself.*

46. How can sickness result in a closer relationship to God? _____

    *Sickness often shows us that we are absolutely dependent upon God.*

47. Why did Jesus teach in parables? _____

*Jesus used parables to conceal truth from those who did not want it and*

*to reveal truth to those who did.*

48. Why did Jesus command people not to talk about His healing them? _____

*Jesus did not want to attract great multitudes that were interested only in*

*physical healing.*

49. What was the defect in the faith of the woman with an issue of blood? _____

*The woman believed that touching Jesus' garment would heal her. The woman*

*needed a personal relationship with God.*

50. For what would a Bible student use a concordance? _____

*Bible students can use a concordance to find verses containing a particular word.*

## True/False

_____ 1. Peter wrote two epistles in the New Testament.

_____ 2. The Sadducees ceased to exist after Christ's Resurrection.

_____ 3. Early believers used a fish symbol to identify themselves.

_____ 4. A young girl identified Peter as a disciple of Christ at His trial.

_____ 5. Jesus' purpose for feeding the four thousand was to teach the disciples patience.

_____ 6. Salt was often used as a preservative.

_____ 7. Commentaries often supply cultural details.

_____ 8. Levi and Matthew are the same person.

_____ 9. Eternal values motivate discipleship.

_____ 10. Moses appeared with Jesus at the Resurrection.

_____ 11. Jesus spoke to the man with a withered hand to heal him.

_____ 12. Jesus rode a young horse into Jerusalem.

_____ 13. Sodom is a symbol of God's judgment on sin.

_____ 14. Leaven is a symbol of wholesome growth.

_____ 15. Christians must meditate in a seated position with their eyes closed.

## Multiple Choice

Choose the best answer.

_____ 16. How many times per year did Moses' law command fasting?

A. 0          D. 3
B. 1          E. 4
C. 2

_____ 17. Which disciple is not identified as a fisherman?

A. Simon          D. Andrew
B. James          E. John
C. Barnabas

_____ 18. What did Jesus curse to teach a lesson on faith?

A. fig tree          D. wheat field
B. grape vine          E. none of the above
C. olive tree

Name _____

_____ 19. Modern methods of spreading the gospel include

A. giving your personal testimony.     D. all of the above
B. handing out gospel tracts.          E. none of the above
C. using the Romans Road.

_____ 20. The group that did not believe in the resurrection from the dead was the

A. Pharisees.     D. priests.
B. Sadducees.     E. Essenes.
C. scribes.

_____ 21. Jesus used the word *offend* to mean

A. eating with poor table manners.     D. speaking rudely.
B. breaking traditions.                E. none of the above
C. causing to sin.

_____ 22. To whom did Jesus say, "Get thee behind me, Satan"?

A. Satan     D. Herod
B. Pilate    E. none of the above
C. Jairus

_____ 23. Jesus connected the ministry of John the Baptist with the ministry of

A. Elijah     D. Moses
B. Elisha     E. Isaiah
C. Aaron

_____ 24. The Old Testament prohibited work on the Sabbath to

A. minimize economic growth.     D. establish the Jewish calendar.
B. imitate other cultures.       E. none of the above
C. encourage physical rest.

_____ 25. What prophet did Jesus quote when the religious leaders confronted Him about hand washing?

A. Isaiah       D. Daniel
B. Jeremiah     E. Malachi
C. Ezekiel

## Matching

Choose the correct answer from the list.

| | |
|---|---|
| A. Law experts | D. Temple worship |
| B. Oral traditions | E. 70 rulers |
| C. Sent one | F. Only in New Testament |

_____ 26. Sanhedrin

_____ 27. Scribes

_____ 28. Herodians

_____ 29. Sadducees

_____ 30. Pharisees

## Short Answer

Write the answer in the space provided.

31. What small action did Jesus say would be rewarded by God? _____

32. According to the scribes, who could forgive sins? _____

33. What did the disciples argue about when Jesus told them about His death? _____

_____

34. Who ate sacred bread reserved for the priests? _____

35. What is worth more than all the material possessions in the world? _____

36. Which disciple said, "Thou art the Christ"? _____

37. Which commandment did the Pharisees break when they gave their money at the temple?

_____

38. What was Jesus doing just prior to walking on the water? _____

39. Who built the temple used during Christ's lifetime? _____

40. At the calming of the sea, the words *be still* mean what? _____

## Essay

Write one or two complete sentences to answer each question.

41. What was the significance of blood in the Old Testament? _____

_____

_____

42. Why did Jesus not choose religious leaders for His disciples? _____

_____

_____

43. What attracted people to Jesus' teachings? _____

_____

_____

44. What was Jesus' purpose in eating with the publicans? _____

_____

_____

45. Why did Jesus send the disciples to teach in the villages? _____

_____

_____

46. What was Jesus' purpose in removing the merchants from the temple? _____

_____

_____

_____

47. How did the transfiguration confirm Jesus' teaching about His death? _____

_____

_____

_____

48. According to Jesus, what was the source of the Pharisees' defective religion? _____

_____

_____

_____

49. How did the religious leaders make money at the temple? _____

_____

_____

_____

50. What defiles a man according to Jesus? _____

_____

_____

## True/False

_**T**_   1. Peter wrote two epistles in the New Testament.

_**F**_   2. The Sadducees ceased to exist after Christ's Resurrection.

_**T**_   3. Early believers used a fish symbol to identify themselves.

_**T**_   4. A young girl identified Peter as a disciple of Christ at His trial.

_**F**_   5. Jesus' purpose for feeding the four thousand was to teach the disciples patience.

_**T**_   6. Salt was often used as a preservative.

_**T**_   7. Commentaries often supply cultural details.

_**T**_   8. Levi and Matthew are the same person.

_**T**_   9. Eternal values motivate discipleship.

_**F**_   10. Moses appeared with Jesus at the Resurrection.

_**T**_   11. Jesus spoke to the man with a withered hand to heal him.

_**F**_   12. Jesus rode a young horse into Jerusalem.

_**T**_   13. Sodom is a symbol of God's judgment on sin.

_**F**_   14. Leaven is a symbol of wholesome growth.

_**F**_   15. Christians must meditate in a seated position with their eyes closed.

## Multiple Choice

Choose the best answer.

_**B**_   16. How many times per year did Moses' law command fasting?

        A. 0                       D. 3
        B. 1                       E. 4
        C. 2

_**C**_   17. Which disciple is not identified as a fisherman?

        A. Simon                D. Andrew
        B. James                E. John
        C. Barnabas

_**A**_   18. What did Jesus curse to teach a lesson on faith?

        A. fig tree             D. wheat field
        B. grape vine         E. none of the above
        C. olive tree

___D___  19. Modern methods of spreading the gospel include

    A. giving your personal testimony.    D. all of the above
    B. handing out gospel tracts.    E. none of the above
    C. using the Romans Road.

___B___  20. The group that did not believe in the resurrection from the dead was the

    A. Pharisees.    D. priests.
    B. Sadducees.    E. Essenes.
    C. scribes.

___C___  21. Jesus used the word *offend* to mean

    A. eating with poor table manners.    D. speaking rudely.
    B. breaking traditions.    E. none of the above
    C. causing to sin.

___E___  22. To whom did Jesus say, "Get thee behind me, Satan"?

    A. Satan    D. Herod
    B. Pilate    E. none of the above
    C. Jairus

___A___  23. Jesus connected the ministry of John the Baptist with the ministry of

    A. Elijah    D. Moses
    B. Elisha    E. Isaiah
    C. Aaron

___C___  24. The Old Testament prohibited work on the Sabbath to

    A. minimize economic growth.    D. establish the Jewish calendar.
    B. imitate other cultures.    E. none of the above
    C. encourage physical rest.

___A___  25. What prophet did Jesus quote when the religious leaders confronted Him about hand washing?

    A. Isaiah    D. Daniel
    B. Jeremiah    E. Malachi
    C. Ezekiel

# TEST 2

## Matching

Choose the correct answer from the list.

A. Law experts
B. Oral traditions
C. Sent one

D. Temple worship
E. 70 rulers
F. Only in New Testament

___E___ 26. Sanhedrin

___A___ 27. Scribes

___F___ 28. Herodians

___D___ 29. Sadducees

___B___ 30. Pharisees

## Short Answer

Write the answer in the space provided.

31. What small action did Jesus say would be rewarded by God? ___Giving a disciple a cup of water___

32. According to the scribes, who could forgive sins? ___God___

33. What did the disciples argue about when Jesus told them about His death? ___Who would be the greatest___

34. Who ate sacred bread reserved for the priests? ___David___

35. What is worth more than all the material possessions in the world? ___A man's soul___

36. Which disciple said, "Thou art the Christ"? ___Peter___

37. Which commandment did the Pharisees break when they gave their money at the temple?

___The fifth, "Honor thy father and thy mother"___

38. What was Jesus doing just prior to walking on the water? ___Praying on a mountain___

39. Who built the temple used during Christ's lifetime? ___Herod the Great___

40. At the calming of the sea, the words *be still* mean what? ___Be muzzled___

**Essay**

Write one or two complete sentences to answer each question.

41. What was the significance of blood in the Old Testament? _____

    ***Blood was used to seal covenants and as a sacrifice for sins.*** _____

    _____

42. Why did Jesus not choose religious leaders for His disciples? _____

    ***The religious leaders did not respond to Christ's teachings.*** _____

    _____

43. What attracted people to Jesus' teachings? _____

    ***People listened to Christ because His words reflected great power, unlike the***

    ***words of the religious leaders.*** _____

44. What was Jesus' purpose in eating with the publicans? _____

    ***Jesus wanted to preach to people who were excluded from Jewish society.*** ___

    _____

45. Why did Jesus send the disciples to teach in the villages? _____

    ***Jesus sent the disciples to preach in more villages and to allow them to learn***

    ***by doing.*** _____

46. What was Jesus' purpose in removing the merchants from the temple? _____

    ***Jesus wanted to restore the temple to its original purpose, which was to be***

    ***a meeting place between God and man.*** _____

47. How did the transfiguration confirm Jesus' teaching about His death? ⎯⎯⎯⎯⎯

   *The transfiguration confirmed Christ's deity and authority; therefore His words about His death should be accepted.*

48. According to Jesus, what was the source of the Pharisees' defective religion? ⎯⎯⎯

   *The Pharisees believed that the oral traditions of the Jews were equal in authority to God's word.*

49. How did the religious leaders make money at the temple? ⎯⎯⎯⎯⎯⎯⎯

   *The leaders exchanged Roman coins for temple coins and also sold items required for sacrifice in order to make money.*

50. What defiles a man according to Jesus? ⎯⎯⎯⎯⎯⎯⎯

   *Jesus said that the things coming out of the heart defile a man.*